We need your help!

Please take a minute to complete return the survey below.

To show our thanks, we'll send you a
free gift
of 30-Minute Meals!

An exclusive collection of 76 kitchen-tested and family-approved meals, with our compliments

D1033260

If you only have 48 hours to redecorate a room, do you have time to cook?

PHOTO of every recipe!

30-Minute meals

76 main dishes • salads soups • desserts

delicious fast
time-savers

---

30 Minute meals

Customer Survey

Things that turn me on:
- ○ Gardening
- ○ Decorating
- ○ Cooking/nutrition
- ○ Health/fitness
- ○ Home improvement
- ○ Crafts
- ○ Quilting
- ○ Travel

How I got this book:
- ○ Discount store
- ○ Membership club
- ○ Home improvement store
- ○ Bookstore
- ○ Internet
- ○ Gift
- ○ Other _____

In the next 6 months I intend to:
- ○ Move
- ○ Redecorate
- ○ Remodel
- ○ Build
- ○ Landscape/improve garden
- ○ Get married/start a family
- ○ Expand my spiritual life
- ○ Start diet/fitness program

Hurry! To get your **free** gift of **30-Minute Meals**, detach and mail this survey today!

Yes!
○ I've completed your survey. Send me a **free gift** of **30-Minute Meals**! I'll mail this today because I know supplies are limited!

Yes!
○ I've completed your survey, but don't want to take advantage of this exclusive free-gift offer.

_____
Name *(Please print)*

_____
Address   Apt. #

_____
City

_____
State   Zip

Please e-mail items of interest to me.

E-mail address: _____

Thank you for completing the survey!

Your gift will mail in 6-8 weeks.
TSBTSF

Two rooms. Two designers. One carpenter. Two sets of homeowners. Two days. And a $1,000 budget.

Trading Spaces
BEHIND THE SCENES

Editor: Brian Kramer
Senior Associate Design Director: Ken Carlson
Contributing Writers: Karin Baji Holmes, Kris Kennedy
Contributing Editors: Vicki L. Ingham, Amy Tincher-Durik
Portrait Photographer: Pam Francis
Contributing Photographers: Janet Mesic Mackie, T. Miyasaki, Alise O'Brien,
  Danny Piassick, Paul Whicheloe (Anyway Productions Inc.)
Cover Photographer: F. Scott Schafer
Copy Chief: Terri Fredrickson
Copy and Production Editor: Victoria Forlini
Editorial Operations Manager: Karen Schirm
Managers, Book Production: Pam Kvitne, Marjorie J. Schenkelberg, Rick Vonholdt
Contributing Researcher: Kellie Kramer
Contributing Copy Editor: Jane Woychick
Contributing Proofreaders: Maria Duryée, Heidi Johnson, Gretchen Kauffman
Electronic Production Coordinator: Paula Forest
Editorial and Design Assistants: Kaye Chabot, Karen McFadden, Mary Lee Gavin

Meredith₀ Books
Editor in Chief: Linda Raglan Cunningham
Design Director and Contributing Photographer: Matt Strelecki
Executive Editor, Home Decorating and Design: Denise L. Caringer

Publisher: James D. Blume
Executive Director, Marketing: Jeffrey Myers
Executive Director, New Business Development: Todd M. Davis
Executive Director, Sales: Ken Zagor
Director, Operations: George A. Susral
Director, Production: Douglas M. Johnston
Business Director: Jim Leonard

Vice President and General Manager: Douglas J. Guendel

Meredith Publishing Group
President, Publishing Group: Stephen M. Lacy
Vice President-Publishing Director: Bob Mate

Meredith Corporation
Chairman and Chief Executive Officer: William T. Kerr

Chairman of the Executive Committee: E. T. Meredith III

Special thanks to everyone who made this book possible, including Robert Bradford,
The Salk Institute for Biological Studies; Le Souk Restaurant, New York City;
David Burrola, Sanctuary Camelback Mountain; Jennifer Dixon, IMS Marketing;
Bob Tucker, Seaworld; Christi Elizabeth; Deborah W. and Josh B., Indy Anna's
Catering; Anne Marie E. and John L.; Kelle R.; "Fast" Eddie Barnard; Gary F., Cindy B.,
Natalie F., Laura S., Kevin M., Daniel S., Marc Jeff S., Mark G., Larry B., Mindy K.,
and Jeff W., Banyan Productions; and all the cool but very tired homeowners.

**Dress worn by Paige Davis from the Broadway production of *Chicago* furnished by the
Chicago Limited Partnership. Dress designed by William Ivey Long.**

All of us at Meredith Books are dedicated to providing you with information and ideas
to enhance your home. We welcome your comments and suggestions. Write to us at:
Meredith Books, Home Decorating and Design Editorial Department, 1716 Locust St.,
Des Moines, IA 50309-3023.

If you would like to purchase any of our home decorating and design, cooking, crafts,
gardening, or home improvement books, check wherever quality books are sold.
Or visit us at: meredithbooks.com

***Trading Spaces* Book Development Team**
Stephen Schwartz, Executive Producer, *Trading Spaces*
Roger Marmet, Vice President, Programming, TLC
Denise Cramsey, Executive Producer, Banyan Productions
Sharon M. Bennett, Senior Vice President, Strategic Partnerships & Licensing
Carol LeBlanc, Vice President, Licensing
Neal Lieberman, Vice President, Consumer Products Licensing
Elizabeth Bakacs, Creative Director, Strategic Partnerships
Nadia Saah, Director, Licensing
Dana Newbold, Product Development Manager

Trading Spaces

BEHIND THE SCENES

Meredith Books
Des Moines, Iowa

Trading
Spaces

contents

You know the drill:

Two rooms. Two designers. One carpenter. Two sets of homeowners. Two days. And a $1,000 budget.

These are The Rules, and they've helped make *Trading Spaces* the top-rated decorating program on cable TV. After three seasons on the air and more than 250 transformed rooms across the United States, the show is as captivating as ever, offering viewers the thrill of watching decorating schemes come together—or blow apart—on each episode.

For skeptics and die-hard fans alike, a host of questions linger: How do homeowners really feel about being part of the creative madness of the show?

Do those daring decorators get along or do paintbrushes go flying once the cameras are turned off? And most important, do they actually redo two rooms in a mere two days, with only two designers, a carpenter, and $1,000?

The answer to that last question is, of course, no. This is television after all! An unseen assistant carpenter helps Amy Wynn or Ty build those elaborate bookcases and storage benches; a sewing coordinator (usually

On the set, there's no time for glamour or prima donna TV star treatment. The *Trading Spaces* cast are regular people who put their pants on one leg at a time—and usually they've had to iron the pants themselves only moments before the shoot.

stitching away in the garage of one of the homes) skillfully pieces together the fabulous fabric projects begun by the cast on-air; a small team of production assistants (who are recruited for each location) tackles tasks, large and small, with astounding zeal; the cost of certain supplies, such as rollers and paint trays, isn't calculated in the $1,000 price tag for a room redo.

But *Trading Spaces* is still "reality TV," filmed in real time and unfolding on-camera so that viewers see the rooms changing right before their eyes. Although each episode has standard elements, such as Homework and The Reveals, the cast and crew—like the viewing audience—have little idea where an episode will lead. Each show creates itself moment by moment while the camera crew records as many of those moments as possible. For each episode, story lines and running jokes emerge, and the cast and crew (and eventually the video production editors) must carefully select the scenes, images, and lines

Know the Lingo

Tell MPDP to have Wynn use the MDF.

Calling all ultimate *Trading Spaces* fans! Pump up your *Trading Spaces* vocabulary with some backstage lingo:

Bumper shots/scenes: Those goofy two-second scenes that come right before and after commercial breaks.

Carpentry World: The trailer and the surrounding area where carpenters Ty and Amy Wynn (and occasionally a homeowner or two) saw, drill, hammer, and build carpentry projects. Carpentry World also is known as "Ty Land" or "Wynn World."

Ceiling fan: An efficient but apparently uncool room-cooling device that is frequently removed by *Trading Spaces* designers.

Day 0: The day filming begins for each episode. The Opener is filmed; then the cast goes shopping and gets ready for the following two days of redecorating (conveniently referred to as Day I and Day 2).

Designer Chat: Paige's up-close-and-personal discussion with each designer after the redecorating is done. The chat happens immediately before The Reveal.

Faux: French for false. *Trading Spaces* designers stick "faux" in front of almost any noun: faux fur, faux marble....

Homework: Projects that the designers assign the homeowners at the end of Day I.

Key Swap: The scene in which Paige crosses her arms and gives each set of homeowners the keys to each other's home so they can trade spaces.

Load Out/Load In: The process of removing a room's old furniture or bringing in all the new projects. Both are usually shown as sped-up footage.

MDF (Medium-density fiberboard): Made of compressed wood pulp and glue, MDF is low cost and paintable, so *Trading Spaces* designers and carpenters often use it to build furniture and shelving.

MPDP: Paige Davis's initials. Her real name is Mindy Paige Davis. She recently married Patrick Page, so her full name is Mindy Paige Davis Page.

The Opener: The first segment of the show, beginning with Paige saying, "Welcome to *Trading Spaces* ...." Classic openers have included spins around the Indianapolis Motor Speedway, trampoline jumping, and horseback riding.

The Overhead: A video camera mounted in an upper corner of each featured room. It records images that can be edited into the final show.

PaigeCam: A handheld camera that Paige uses to film designers and homeowners hard at work on projects.

The Reveal: The act of showing the homeowners their redone rooms. A true *Trading Spaces* junkie might say, "Did you catch last night's Reveal? Man, there were some tears!"

Sewing World: An area, often in the garage of one of the homes, where all fabric projects—sewing, upholstering, ironing, pillow stuffing, and more—happen.

Straw: First in a growing list of Hildi's infamous wallcovering materials. Other Hildi wallcovering choices have included record albums, wine bottle labels, and silk flowers.

that best distill 48 hours of furious activity into 1 hour of riveting television.

The realities of creating an episode of *Trading Spaces* offer lessons that help do-it-yourself decorators take heart. The best lesson? Flexibility and improvisation are often more valuable than decorating know-how when it comes to completing a redecorating project. Detailed design plans are great, but being able to creatively adapt to a shrinking budget and disappearing time is even better. Not enough money to buy oak legs for an end table? Make a funky set from fluorescent plastic tumblers. Can't muster the courage to dye your carpet orange? Sprinkle coral-color silk rose petals around the room. Can't afford to reupholster the furniture? If you're willing to gamble, spray-paint it! Need quick art? Frame colorful snippets of tissue paper.

The reactions, the time crunch, the dramas, the traumas—all are real. So is the hard work. The cast, homeowners, producers, sound and

Making an Episode

Dying to know what's really going on behind the CAUTION tape? Read on to find out just how an episode of *Trading Spaces* goes together.

Start

Sign Up: Interested homeowners sign up online at www.tlc.com. Rooms should be at least 14'×12'. Relationship discord is not allowed, and homeowners must be willing to sign away any right to sue for things they don't like.

Screening: Potential homeowners are thoroughly screened. The best way to be selected is to act like your goofy self. For example, one homeowner couple wore T-shirts featuring large silk-screen noses and the phrase "Pick us."

Match-Up: Designers are matched up with rooms (and no, you can't pick your designer). With only a handful of photos of the selected room and a 20-minute video of the homeowners, the designers have two to three weeks to figure out their design plans and how to achieve them in a distant location.

Paint Reveal: The spontaneous slapping of paint onto walls is actually a carefully calculated shot. By noon, most rooms already have a first coat of paint, and the main carpentry or sewing projects have begun.

Load Out: The designer and homeowners miraculously clear an entire room in 30 seconds or less. (Production assistants carry off items and put them into temporary storage in a spare bedroom or garage. Amazingly, the entire process takes only about 15 minutes.)

Meet-and-Greet: The homeowners describe what they'd like to see happen in their neighbors' room, and then the designers tell the homeowners what they're planning to do. If there's going to be tension between the designers and homeowners, it'll start popping up about now.

Day 2

Special Segments: Sewing, painting, building, or arts and crafts projects can take 45 minutes to an hour to film. Why? Often a project is filmed several times. Attention may be focused on different aspects of the project, verbal instructions, or details regarding hands, tools, and materials.

Homework: On-camera it may appear as if the designer is leaving for the night; in reality, most of the cast and crew stay to help the homeowners complete the assigned tasks.

More Work: Designers meet with their homeowners to discuss what did (and didn't) get done the previous evening. Time and work usually begin to wear on the homeowners at this point. Paige assesses the homeowners' mental and physical condition.

8

camera technicians, makeup assistants, and many more work incredibly hard. Designers Vern Yip and Frank Bielec have been noted for putting in extra hours on their projects during certain episodes, but they're not alone in their devotion. Other cast and crew members often work late into the night on the homeowners' homework assignments—all because they're passionate about making good television and about producing dramatic decorating transformations.

This book is your backstage pass, taking you beyond the yellow security tape and the video cameras and into the creative minds of your favorite designers and carpenters. Get ready to hang out with the cast and crew, discover the personal side of each member of this ragtag bunch, and get swept up in the excitement (and, yes, hard work) of transforming a space. Along the way, you'll find advice, inspiring ideas, and insider tricks that will help you make your own inexpensive yet dramatic changes.

The time for a change is now. So, in the words of host Paige Davis, "Let's trade spaces!"

Overhead cam

TION **CAUTION** **CAUTION** **CAUTION** **CAUTION** **CAUTION**

Day 0

Arrival: The *Trading Spaces* crew rolls into town. You may be watching for a caravan of decorating superstars; what you'll see instead is a travel trailer hooked up to a 4×4 truck. The whole ensemble is about the size of a trailer you'd choose to move from your first apartment.

Filming begins: The cast and crew film all the events that make up the start of a show (called B-Roll), from Paige's first lines to those goofy segments in which the cast horses around at some geographically significant site.

Home Visit: The cast and crew visit the homes. Both designers sit down with the carpenter for the show and hash out what's going to happen during the next two days.

Day 1

Show Time: Bright and early, the homeowners join Paige outside and perform the sacred Key Swap. During breaks, Paige gives the homeowners a pep talk on how to look natural on-camera and how to make the show fun. They often have to do the swap multiple times to get the excitement just right.

Shopping time: The designers and carpenters brave rabid fans, traffic jams, dwindling funds, and a strange, new town in their quest for the wood, paint, hardware, fabric, furniture, and accessories they'll need to transform their spaces.

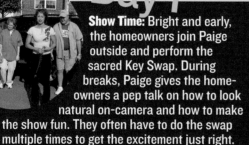

Load In. This is the opposite of Load Out. Regardless of how much time is actually left, Paige films a few "Hurry Up" scenes, in which she pushes designers and homeowners to speedily put on the finishing touches.

Designer Chat: Paige interviews each designer, highlighting the key projects. An associate producer takes notes on what is discussed so Paige can bring up the same topics with the homeowners during The Reveal.

The Reveal: The climax of three days of hard work. Because the homeowners' reactions can't be filmed a second time, lighting, sound, and camera angles must be perfect. Often, cast and crew watch the reactions on a video monitor.

Finish

Who is your design soulmate?

	Doug	Laurie	Genevieve
Signature Style	East Village retro-glam, with traditionalism lurking beneath the surface	Clean-lined classicism and a commitment to symmetry	Reasoned eclecticism: Rooms built on passion for a person, place, or thing
Known for	Groovy living lounges, risky art projects, and making homeowners cry	Fabulous throw pillows, reams of gorgeous fabric, hatred of ceiling fans	Playful love "nests" (literally) and a teenage girl's "No Parents Meditation Zone"
Working Wardrobe	Fitted button-down shirts and occasional leather pants	A blouse to match her color scheme	Black T-shirts, Diesel jeans, big belts, and bubble gum
Budget Blower	Almost anything	Silk, silk, silk	Shipping costs for importing her latest international inspiration
Design Must-Have	A working title for every room	A focal point	Unusually cropped photographs and kindergarten art
Biggest Faux Pas	Stadium seating in a family room	Southern belles don't make faux pas	Moss-covered walls for allergy-suffering homeowners
Stress Reliever	Razor-sharp quips to homeowners	Lamenting with homeowners: "I'm totally freaking out, y'all!"	Rapid arm movements
Decor that would make them cry	Cry?	Ceiling fans, of course	Entertainment centers or anything centered
Celebrity you'd love to see them take on	George Steinbrenner— think battle of wills	The Osbournes	Bert and Ernie

10

Frank	Hildi	Edward	Kia	Vern
Down-home country clutter emphasizing crafts and personal expression	Modern sophistication served with a twist: Fifth Avenue meets Cirque de Soleil	Smartly tailored suburbia with a dollop of neon attitude	"Hey, look at me!" theatricality with a dash of sass	Precisely ordered rooms mixing equal parts dynamism and restraint
Folksy murals, banged-up furniture, and accessorizing with clothespins	Charcoal-colored paint on every surface, straw glue to walls, tenting rooms in fabric	Cording as crown molding, disco/deco light-up beds	Red, white, and blue decor with camouflage accents; the infamous "graveyard" bed	Two-toned rooms and tedious installations
Casual comfort in the form of denim clam-diggers and high-top sneaks	Prada pumps that cost more than the room	See any page from the Banana Republic catalog	Theme jewelry, preferably from the late 1980s	Muscle T-shirts—crisply tailored
Glue sticks and paint	Replacement upholstered furniture after ruining homeowners' sofas	Miles of plush red velvet	A funky pod racer from the set of *Star Wars, Episode I*	Nothing –always gets "an incredible deal"
Chickens	Chocolate brown paint	A glue gun	Artsy arrangement of dunk-and-stick wallpaper border	A straightedge ruler
It's a tie: naming pig art or adding handcuffs to Grandma's rocker	Felt-upholstered walls for a home with three cats	The verdict's still out—he hasn't really screwed up yet	That smelly, leaky pyramid fountain	*Feng shui* mirrors on a first-floor ceiling
Perspiration	Machine-gun stapling	Force-stuffing pillows	Getting some distance from the homeowners	Working even harder
Midcentury minimalism	White	Anything over the top	Anything subtle and understated	Faux anything and curlicues
Doug Wilson—just to see him cry	Jackie Collins	Courtney Love (with or without Hole)	Madonna—all incarnations	Bill Gates

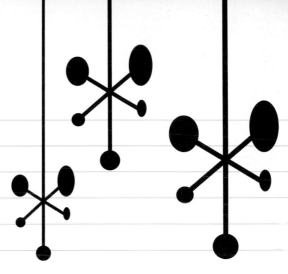

> **"I am never ever faking it when I walk in and say, 'This room is never going to get done.' I'm a natural worrywart. I always think things are going to go wrong.**

Hi. Welcome to Paige Davis, the host of cable TV's most popular decorating show and the portrayer of emotional reactions so pure and direct—enthusiasm, tension, amazement—that fans of the show might wonder if the emotions are real.

Rest assured: They are. "I feel things that intensely all the time," says Paige. "I feel that sad and that elated and that excited." By training, Paige is a musical theater actress, but if you think her highs and lows on *Trading Spaces* are an act, think again. "I definitely get hurt when it's assumed that any of that emotion is fake," she says. "I am never ever faking it when I walk in and say, 'This room is never going to get done.' I'm a natural

paige davis

worrywart. I always think things are going to go wrong."

The host seen on TV is smiling, bouncing, dancing, spinning, and Paige concedes that she is usually as people describe her: perky, bubbly, sensitive. "I bring a positive energy to the show," she says. She has that Julia Roberts or Kelly Ripa girl-next-door quality that makes her approachable and comfortable to be around. While she was eating in an Indiana hotel restaurant one night, several patrons struck up conversations with her. They told Paige they were staying in the hotel because their homes had been destroyed in a tornado the week before. This is the kind of thing that stabs Paige in the heart. Unable to do

Ever since she memorized all the parts in *West Side Story* at age 13, Paige has been passionate about musical theater. Favorite roles include Babette, the French feather duster, in *Beauty and the Beast* and being the understudy for Roxie in *Chicago*.

13

Fashion Statement

A big part of Paige's job is shopping. She's responsible for getting her own on-camera outfits, which usually consist of chunky boots, low-rise jeans, and tight-fitting shirts that feature sparkles, feathers, or slogans. "I have a budget and in between interviews, filming, and other hosting responsibilities, I have to find time to visit the mall," she says. She'll try on dozens of shirts to find one or two that work. Not only do they need to look good, of course, but they must also work for the camera, with her jeans, and with a microphone. She has to be able to fold them up and pack them in the plastic bins she lugs from shoot to shoot. And she needs a lot of them, because once she's worn a shirt on one episode, she's not allowed to wear it again. She looks for shirts that are unique and will try to match a shirt to a show, either in color or theme. Sometimes an even bigger challenge is making one shirt last the whole episode. The cast members often wear the same outfit three days in a row (Days 0, 1, and 2) so scenes will be easier to edit. When a shirt gets ruined, everyone panics. In Rhode Island she spilled salad dressing on her Gap camouflage tank top. The film crew already had her on-camera wearing the top, but they still needed to shoot the first scene. Production assistants called every Gap in the state. The store at the opposite end of the state had one tank top in Paige's size, so someone had to drive there and pick it up before shooting could resume.

You want me to paint *what* green?

more, she used her less-than-celebrity pay to buy them all a round of drinks. Paige smiles a lot, but that expression can be misleading. She tells even sad stories (her grandmother's death, failed relationships) with a smile on her face, and her stories are so heartfelt they give you goosebumps. Paige's fretting over the schedule and budget, her pride in the rooms, her nervousness during The Reveal, her tenderness when homeowners don't like their room

Paige and her first four-legged best friend, Sandy

are natural qualities that make her a great host for a reality show. On *Trading Spaces*, Paige is us. She feels astounded or disappointed right along with the television viewers, and on their behalf she gets to say what she's thinking, whether she's commiserating with homeowners over something that looks bad or expressing consternation when the designers have hit Amy Wynn with way too many projects. "This is very different from being an actress," she says of her host job. "My success on the show really depends on people liking *me*." Because it's a reality show, she doesn't have the luxury of escaping into a fictional character's skin.

Paige's emotional range and guilelessness have helped her succeed as an actress and a host, but these qualities haven't always played a positive role in her personal life. She contends that people rarely feel ambivalent about her. They either love her because they think she's a positive life force that lights up a

> **"This is very different from being an actress. My success on the show really depends on people liking *me*. *Trading Spaces* has affected me on a personal level because I absolutely positively had to become comfortable with just being myself.**

room, or they hate her because they find her, as Paige puts it, "loud, obnoxious, dramatic, overbearing, and annoying."

Though she's now famous for her peppy personality, Paige was not the cheerleader type in school. "I was very nerdy and unsure of myself," she confides. "I was teased and mocked a lot." She found refuge onstage, first in grade school as an on-camera personality for a kids' TV show produced in Madison, Wisconsin. She also did gymnastics and competed at the state level until age 13. Around that time she found her mother's

West Side Story album. She played the album and acted out all the parts, again and again. A musical theater career became her all-consuming ambition.

After her parents' divorce, Paige and her younger sister moved with their mother and stepfather to Louisville, Kentucky, where Paige attended the Youth Performing Arts School, choosing a concentration in dance. "From 14 on I knew without a doubt that's what I wanted to do," she says. "I felt more happy and uplifted and satisfied and thrilled when I was dancing than anything else I'd ever done." The school

Paige spends a lot of time off-camera prepping the homeowners on what to expect. On-camera, she spells out the rules of the game before handing over the keys.

> **From 14 on, I knew dancing was what I wanted to do. I felt more happy and uplifted and satisfied and thrilled when I was dancing than anything else I'd ever done.**

also put her in contact with like minds. Paige remembers the fun and relief that atmosphere brought her: "Suddenly I had all these other people around me who were just as colorful and loud and weird as I was. I was kind of normal." She spent summers with her father and stepmother, going to day camps in New Jersey, where she also studied theater and dance.

Paige in a high school performance of *West Side Story*

Paige carried on her schedule of two dance classes a day, five days a week, through college. She attended the Meadows School of the Arts at Southern Methodist University, choosing SMU because she wanted the intellectual breadth of a liberal arts college, but her passion lay in her performance classes. "It was my intention at all times that I would move to New York and start a musical theater career on Broadway." During her senior year, however, she met a fellow student in temple on Yom Kippur, and the relationship took her to L.A. After five years the couple wed, but the marriage lasted less than a year because, says Paige, she was too young and didn't know herself or what she wanted.

Professionally, Paige landed the first part she auditioned for, a role in a regional production of *Hello, Dolly!* starring Nell Carter and Nipsey

Paige at age 4 or 5 with her grandmother. Television viewers who saw Paige's nuptials in *A Wedding Story* learned how Paige became her dying grandmother's caregiver.

Russell. On dress rehearsal night she slipped out of her shoe and injured her ankle. During her recovery, she worked for the orthopedic surgeon who treated her, and when her ankle finally healed, she took work where she could get it: dancing at L.A. Gear conventions and Shaklee conventions, which took her to Hawaii, Europe, and the Caribbean; singing and dancing with the Bob Gail Orchestra at weddings and bar mitzvahs; starring in karaoke videos that Paige speculates are still playing in Japan; doing TV commercials; and backup dancing for a Beach Boys tour. "For me, L.A. was going from a gig to a gig to a gig," she says.

Moment to Moment

What's life like on the road with *Trading Spaces*? We called Paige on her cell phone to find out.

Sunday 11:45 a.m.

I'm putting on fishnets. I'm in a Los Angeles sound studio in the dressing room that time forgot. It's all decorated really funny, like Baroque, just really too much. I'm about to do a musical Paige-tacular to promote the live Las Vegas Reveal, and my six dancing boys are waiting for me to finish getting into costume. The set features a flight of stairs leading to a lit-up *Trading Spaces* sign, and I'm in a feathered costume, à la *Moulin Rouge*. I laid down the vocal track the other day, so I'll be lip-synching my heart out.

Monday 4:45 p.m.

I'm on set getting smoothed out by the makeup artist. I've been running around and had lunch, and the makeup has migrated, so it's being brought back north. I'm about to go on-camera to shoot a project with Frank. We're in San Clemente, California, and it's Day I. For lunch, I had tofu, couscous, and salad. I really want some Jell-O, but I haven't had a chance to eat it yet, because when I'm on lunch is also when I make a ton of phone calls.

Wednesday 7:38 a.m.

I just walked in from the hotel gym, where I did the treadmill and Pilates mat work. Today I started at 6 but I usually start at 5. Doing it so early is the lesser of two evils because it's easier than coming home after a 12- or 16-hour day and trying to work out then. I hate working out. I can't stand it. I think it's boring. I hate to get up. But I do it every day for an hour and a half. I have to, to keep any kind of body.

Thursday 1:57 p.m.

I was out late last night. Amy Wynn, Vern, and I had dinner at Patricia Heaton's house in L.A. The stylist who did Amy Wynn for the daytime Emmys also does Patricia sometimes, and Patricia is a huge fan of the show. Her husband kept saying, "I can't believe you're in our house!" It was really cute. I met her four young sons. It was really relaxed. Her assistant is an amazing cook and made us chicken pot pies, butternut squash, and apple soup. Then this morning I drove back to San Diego, and we shot the opener at SeaWorld. I hugged a killer whale! And Vern actually rode a dolphin, hanging on to the fin and everything.

Saturday 7:26 p.m.

I'm in Tampa where Patrick is doing the national tour of *The Lion King*. He's playing Scar. I'm in his furnished corporate apartment, sprawled out and trying to get caught up on all my personal paperwork and affairs. I have to file two months of tax receipts, input addresses into my PalmPilot, pay bills, answer e-mail. I need to leave in 15 minutes to pick up Patrick from the show. We'll come home, and he'll probably have a plate of sliced tomatoes (his favorite food), baby carrots, and pepperoncinis and be dripping onto the floor with me hovering over him. I often walk 6 inches behind him cleaning up after him as he goes.

paige davis

Born: October 15, 1969

Raised: Pennsylvania, Virginia, Wisconsin, Kentucky, New Jersey

Adopted Hometown: The road. Paige spends about 20 days a month shooting *Trading Spaces*. During her off-time she flies to wherever her husband, Patrick, is performing (he's an actor). They have a small apartment in Manhattan, but they're never there. Says Paige, "I'm basically for the whole year just traveling with three suitcases."

Hobby: Politics. "It's like my sports. When Patrick and I have been apart, we've often stayed on the phone with each other during the entire State of the Union address."

Photographed in Dallas, Texas on October 20, 2002.

Crunch Time: While everyone else freezes for 30 seconds of silence for sound recording, Paige lies down on the bathroom floor and starts doing stomach crunches. She's quiet. She doesn't seem to notice that everyone is looking at her.

It was in L.A., though, where she finally landed a major-league part, as Center Plate in the national tour of *Beauty and the Beast*. "I was told it was coveted and I chose to believe it," she says, laughing. *Beauty and the Beast* is also where she met her future husband, Patrick Page, who played Lumière the candelabra. Fifteen months later, Paige took over the role of Babette the French feather duster. "I was finally living my dream," she says. After a tour of more than two years, Paige spent some time living in Manhattan before landing the role of one of the merry murderesses in the show *Chicago*. She appeared first in the national tour, then in the Broadway company, and finally in the company that went to Portugal. She also understudied the part of Roxie and still catches her breath at the thought of performing opposite Ben Vereen. Says Paige of her *Chicago* experience, "Even

Paige and Patrick in their *Beauty and the Beast* costumes

with *Trading Spaces* on the plate, that's still the career highlight of my life."

Hosting a cable TV decorating show seemed way out in left field for the up-and-coming Broadway star, and that must have been what the *Trading Spaces* producers thought too when Paige

20

What Paige Has Learned About Design

Paige thought her Manhattan apartment, with its antique-gold living room and sage green bedroom, was pretty cute ...

...until she started hosting *Trading Spaces*. "When I look at my apartment now, I just see predictability," she says. "I used to say I was 'romantic contemporary.' I'm so over that." From her castmates, Paige has learned at least one key to good design; she puts it like this: "Be brave. If you have a thought, just go with it." And, she adds, "Do not be afraid of color." She's ready for some new color herself and can't wait to try Genevieve's rust wall technique, which involves oxidizing metallic paint (but, of course, she'll have to wait until she settles down again).

Paige understands why people make safe choices. They have limited budgets and tightly scheduled free time, so they can't afford to redecorate if they hate the results of their first attempt. But Paige says, even though *Trading Spaces* redecorates a room in two days, you don't need to rush your design ideas. "Wait and savor the pieces and artifacts and surprises that find you," she says. She also advises against copying exact looks from the show. Instead, use the ideas as a springboard; as Paige says, "Let it be organic and let it really be you."

relentlessly lobbied them for an audition. Her good friend Risa, a producer for *A Wedding Story*, thought Paige would be perfect for *Trading Spaces* and insisted she give it a try. Paige submitted her resume. Heard nothing. Called. The producers said they weren't interested. Paige then got her agent to write the producers a letter, and she won a spot during the last day of auditions. "I had no notion of being cast at all," says Paige, who merely wanted the production company to know who she was.

For the audition, Paige was asked to do a show opener; then the producers had her do a scene with Ty, in which they pretended to be working on a mantel. "I think one of the biggest mistakes the other girls made was talking about the mantel," Paige says.

While shooting in Indiana, the cast trooped out to a farm to film footage for the show's opening scenes. Paige tried her hand at milking a cow but preferred bottle-feeding a calf.

Off Broadway: Paige had to lobby hard to persuade the *Trading Spaces* producers to give her an audition, but she eventually clawed her way in, she says. "I always say I still have the blood under my fingernails," she jokes.

Paige was familiar with the show and intrigued with the concept. She also knew a TV gig would be great exposure for her. Her goal was to be able to go back to Broadway and, instead of being the understudy, be the lead. "That's the big joke," she says, "that you have to do TV to do theater."

The popularity of the show, however, has opened up more and different opportunities than she had anticipated. Her fame has its little perks too. At an Indiana eatery, Paige gets dinner for free because the floor manager's wife loves the show. While shooting an episode on the U.S. Air Force base in Missouri, she hits it off with

General Handy, who arranges for Paige and Patrick to fly in a refueling jet in Tampa. "My family calls that 'The Paige Power,'" she says.

Paige's "host" title doesn't fully encompass what she does on the show. She isn't merely an on-camera face who lolls around between shots. On set, she's also a garbage collector, project maker, mediator, and people manager. Perhaps because she's moved around so much in her life, Paige feels compelled to maintain order around her. She's a bit of a neatnik and will grab empty beverage cups as she glides through rooms. More frequently, you'll see her off by herself completing a project, though no one has asked her to. She might be stapling upholstered panels, weaving ribbon through chair backs, or hot-gluing beaded trim to lampshades. And

23

Paige takes a moment to meet and greet even her youngest fans.

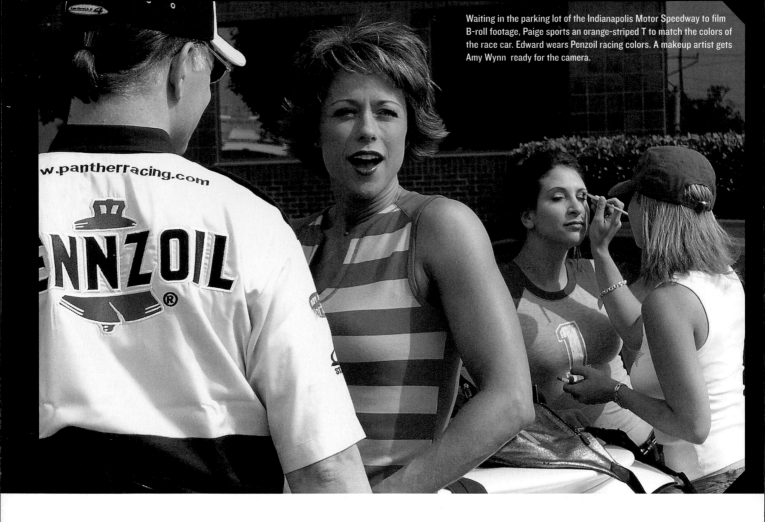

Greatest irony: Paige is both a graceful dancer and a total klutz. "I've woken up in the hospital a number of times, having knocked myself out and given myself a concussion," she says.

usually no one even knows she has done it. She also jumps in to avert crises. Once, toward the end of Day 2, a big carpet spot still needed to be covered. The designer didn't have a rug and didn't have time to get one. Paige grabbed the rest of the budget—about $100 in cash—and drove herself and the homeowner to the store, picked out a rug, and drove like a demon back to the house.

During the filming of an episode, each house has its own designer, producer, and crew; these teams don't mix. Paige, however, flits between the two houses, which gives her a special vantage point as well as added responsibility. She can compare the progress of one room with developments in the other; she can observe running jokes on each set. She sometimes offers ideas for shots, pointing out what might be

Paige helps implement Vern's idea for artwork.

funny in relation to what's going on at the other house. She decides what to shoot for PaigeCam and often has her little camera in hand.

Paige's people skills make her a natural for ensuring that things run smoothly. When the *Trading Spaces*

24

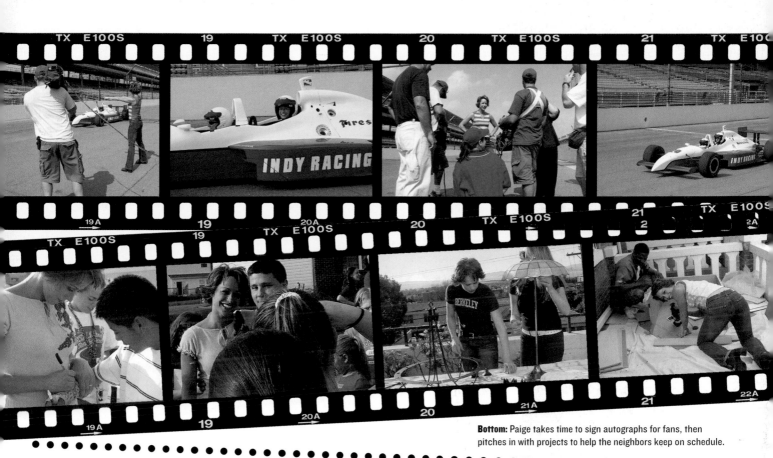

truck shows up and the two home invasions begin, the homeowners don't know exactly what to expect and may feel cast aside. Paige spends much of her time making them feel comfortable. The designers, carpenters, and crew may change from location to location, but Paige is there for every episode—familiar, comforting; she knows, perhaps better than anyone, exactly what's going on. Shortly before The Reveals, when anticipation and tensions run high, she sits down with each set of homeowners and methodically explains what they can expect. She encourages them to express their opinions honestly. Because in the end, when the homeowners walk in and their just-opened eyes are so blinded by the TV lights they can't even see the camera crew, the homeowners aren't talking to America. They're talking to Paige.

What's in a Name? Right, Mindy?

Paige's full name is Mindy Paige Davis, and until *Trading Spaces*, that was her showbiz name too. She likes the name Paige and tacked it onto her first name, so her family and friends still call her Mindy Paige. When she got the *Trading Spaces* job, the producers asked her if "Mindy" was short for anything more mature-sounding. Paige decided to drop her first name. That solved one problem, but it caused another when her boyfriend, Patrick, proposed: His last name is Page. So Paige kept her maiden name. Patrick had always called her Mindy, but for her 32nd birthday, he gave his wife a unique gift: He started calling her Paige. She recalls, "He said, 'You really are a different woman from the woman I met. On your birthday, let's celebrate the birth of this new person.'"

frank bielec

> "I cannot believe I'm still on the show. Let's face it—what chance does a fat, balding, sweaty, middle-age man have on a TV show? It's like Salvador Dalí is orchestrating my life right now."

Somewhere in Texas is a very old, very private woman with a penchant for the Old Testament. She translates biblical stories—Jonah and the whale, the tower of Babel, Cain and Abel—into mixed-media collages, using paint, found objects, torn wallpaper, old fabric, leather, bottle caps, anything. Her work is shown across the country. This wise woman is one of the many faces of Frank Bielec. "I vent my creativity by painting and filling a gallery under a pseudonym," says Frank, who has been a fine artist his whole life. "I needed to invent this person just to get some stuff out of my system."

The unexpected popularity of *Trading Spaces* has left Frank Bielec the Man feeling like Frank Bielec the Commodity. When he does art under his own name, he sees some people buying his work for the signature, not the content. This bugs him. But Frank has no problem throwing back what people dish out, and he decided to give these signature-seekers a little wake-up call. A recent gallery show consisted of 25 canvases, each one featuring nothing but an immense Frank Bielec signature. Frank figures if people want to buy his name, they can.

"I'm more than a chicken painter!" crows Frank Bielec with the help of some newfound poultry pals. While many fans consider him the *Trading Spaces* master of country and kitsch, Frank's overriding passion is comfort.

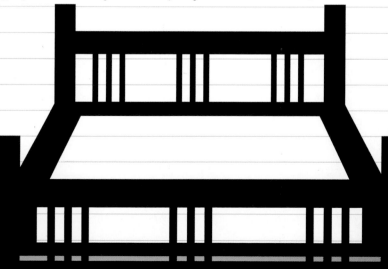

Fans and Frank

Frank gets frank about frightening encounters with fans.

All the *Trading Spaces* cast members say they enjoy interacting with courteous fans; when discussing rude fans, though, most of the cast are more cryptic, not wanting to seem unappreciative of their growing celebrity status. Not Frank; if a fan is rude, he gives it right back. If someone stares at him without saying anything, he stares back. He loves fans who engage him in conversation. He hates it when fans demand things of him, for example, when they demand his autograph instead of asking nicely. And if you shove a cell phone in his face and demand he talk, "You may be eligible for what I call 'Frank's open season on fans,'" he says. "I slump to the floor and go rag-like. I could be in the middle of an airport. I say, 'I have a very sensitive pacemaker, and if you don't get that phone away from me, I'm going to faint.'" People usually run in fear. "It helps pass the time in airports," says Frank.

> " Never in my wildest nightmares did I think I'd do anything in media. My goal has been to have an antiques store and a B&B—and give classes in cross-stitch and decorative painting. "

In the meantime, much of his more thoughtful work is shown under the pseudonym for his older, female alter ego. "She allows me to do things that I would not be allowed to as 'Frank Bielec, *Trading Spaces*,'" he says. "She's getting superb reviews, I might add. We're very pleased. My biggest fear is that they're going to ask her to appear at one of the shows."

Old Woman Gallery Artist is only one of many personas Frank has donned over the years. Others have included Student, Teacher, Artist, Single Guy, Married Guy, Wild Dresser, Florist, Caterer, Philosopher, Cross-Stitch Designer, Hunk, Funny Guy, Homey Guy, and TV Personality. Like the collages he creates, Frank is a mixed-media composition. Over time, different aspects of himself have overlapped, shifted, mutated, taken prominence, or been discarded. Right now, *Trading Spaces* Designer appears to be at the forefront, especially to people who don't know Frank. Ask the man behind the persona, and he'll tell you he loves working on the show and especially likes the "neat and friendly"

Stop me before I "tchotchke" again!

people he gets to work with. But he's quick to point out that *Trading Spaces* is not his whole life. "This is my job," Frank says. "It's no different from a man going off to work at a factory."

While sitting in a subpar hotel room next to a freeway, Frank (wearing a Frida Kahlo T-shirt that Kia gave him, khaki pants, tennis shoes, and

Staple gun in hand, Frank plots his next home decorating move.

28

Frank and his St. Louis team rush to make their deadline—but never forget to have a good time.

a Superman ring) admits a part of him is the folksy-country designer viewers know. Yes, he's the one who builds a dinghy dog bed, nails wooden clouds to the ceiling, and names his weather vane pig Poopalina. Frank is warmly received by viewers who want their rooms to look more like a home than a New York City showroom. Detractors consider his room designs cutesy and disorganized, but Frank feels that the buzz about him, generated largely on the Internet, has put him in an extremely narrow pigeonhole. His cute projects and colorful designs are the ones that stand out in viewers' minds, but an overview of his episodes proves the breadth of his ability: Some of his rooms border on modern. While discussing his

reputation, Frank becomes increasingly fidgety, shifting around in his chair and finally proclaiming, "I'm more than just a chicken painter!"

In person, Frank is a little edgier than you might guess. Much of what he says is funny, but he doesn't laugh that much. He is the same unfailingly polite, encouraging, and solicitous designer you see on the show. However, unlike his designer persona, he is quite opinionated and has much to say about intolerant people, poseurs, the cult of celebrity, media manipulation of American culture, contrived trends in fashion and art, and the one-dimensional assumptions people make about him. "People perceive you to be really interested in design and

> "I have a lot of sides to me, but I basically try to be kind to other people. When I'm criticized for that, it makes me violently upset, but then I decide not to waste my energy, and I move on—to something like a candy bar."

that you sit around and paint cute characters all the time," he says. "And when you're not that person, they're disappointed."

Frank's interior design is more than chickens, and his life is more than interior design. He calls his wife, Judy, his "mooring post" and credits her with making him the person he is today. They operate their own cross-stitch business, called Mosey 'n Me, and live in a small Texas home. Judy is in charge of the home decorating; the house is filled with bleached-out hues, Shaker-style furniture, antique samplers, and lots of plants and flowers.

A voracious reader, Frank effortlessly interlaces his hilarious homespun Frank-isms with quotes from Kierkegaard, Picasso, and Russian-American sculptor Louise Nevelson. Although some of his *Trading Spaces* designs may be lighthearted, he doesn't take art or design lightly. He has a deep interest in and a broad knowledge of American folk crafts. "I really feel that the needle arts and textiles are the only viable art form these days that I find interesting," he says. He's especially drawn to needlepoint, quilting, and other art done by women in the context of their full lives of raising children and working. "I have a lot of sides to me, but I basically try to be kind to other people," he says. "When I'm

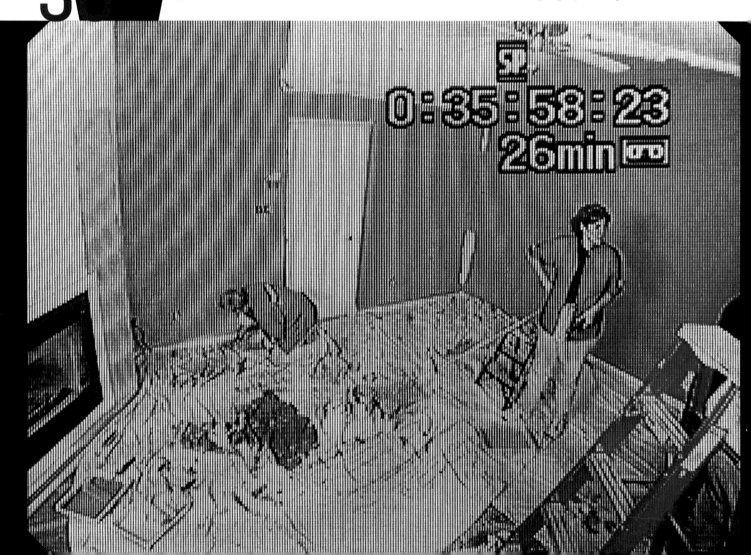

criticized for that, it makes me violently upset, but then I decide not to waste my energy and I move on— to something like a candy bar."

Frank's adult life can be summed up in two strokes: Before Judy and After Judy. As a young man, Before Judy, Frank came by his serious side honestly. He has a bachelor's degree in education, a master of fine arts degree, and a master's in education, all of which he pooh-poohs as not having taught him more than everyday

experience has. Never intending to earn a living through his art, Frank became a teacher. He taught elementary school, then taught secondary school social studies and art. He left teaching after eight years, because it seemed to him that the system no longer educated children but only trained them to take mandated tests. He became a florist and remained in the profession

for 20 years. He credits that job with best preparing him for *Trading Spaces*: "That's the one business that has helped me think on my feet and be organized." All the while, Frank created and sold his art, specializing in large assembled pieces. For one bank lobby, he made a story-and-a-half-high woven piece from aquarium tubing and garbage bags. He calls his early designs "terribly profound," as he shakes his head thinking about himself in his 20s and early 30s. "You think you know so much about life, and it's such a joke."

Something else you should know about Frank during his "profound" period: He fashioned himself a "hottie." He was (and

31

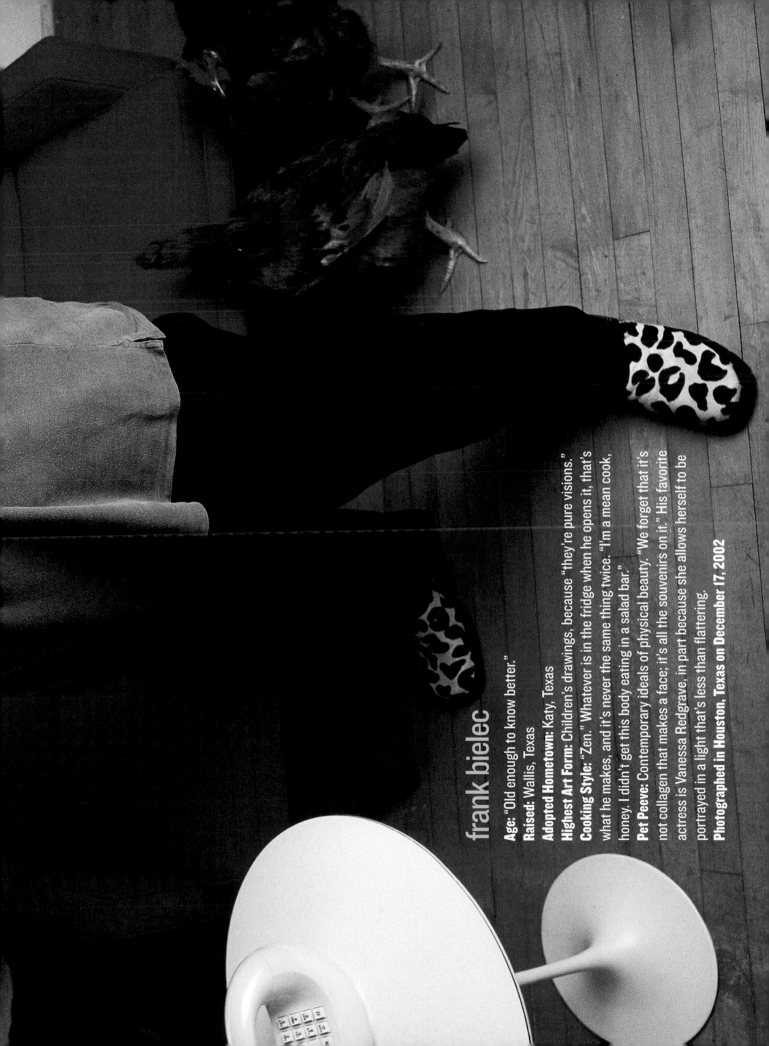

frank bielec

Age: "Old enough to know better."

Raised: Wallis, Texas

Adopted Hometown: Katy, Texas

Highest Art Form: Children's drawings, because "they're pure visions."

Cooking Style: "Zen." Whatever is in the fridge when he opens it, that's what he makes, and it's never the same thing twice. "I'm a mean cook, honey. I didn't get this body eating in a salad bar."

Pet Peeve: Contemporary ideals of physical beauty. "We forget that it's not collagen that makes a face; it's all the souvenirs on it." His favorite actress is Vanessa Redgrave, in part because she allows herself to be portrayed in a light that's less than flattering.

Photographed in Houston, Texas on December 17, 2002

after

before

White master bedroom

Trading Spaces

Frank and his team collaborated on this funky St. Louis-area bedroom. Custom art, whimsical murals, a framed portrait, and a luscious lips-shape headboard add personal touches.

he chokes on these words as he says them) an aerobics instructor. "I was in incredible physical shape at that time. I was a god," he says. In fact, he met Judy when she attended one of his classes. "It was lust at first sight," he says of her great legs. "I was wilder than a March Hare and loved being single." But, eventually, the two friends fell in love, and the demarcation line of Frank's life was drawn.

One day, in his feverish love for this leggy, personally conservative cross-stitcher, Frank drew a cute little bunny on a piece of paper, wrote "I love you" next to it, and put it on the mirror for Judy to see. "For me to draw that bunny was, like, so odd," he

says. "It would make a greeting card look serious—like a Communist poster." Judy decided to turn the bunny drawing into a cross-stitch pattern, and the direction of their lives instantly unfolded before them. Frank started designing cross-stitch patterns, and the couple sold them. "My friends thought it was absolute prostitution that I was doing these

Frank never met a paintbrush he didn't like, or a color he wouldn't try.

bunnies and stuff," he says. "They say, 'He used to be very good.'" Instead of creating "art with a capital A," Frank found value in home and family life and decided to use his talent to support this new existence. "It was a blinding instant of realization that there was not much importance in what I was doing," he says. "I went from being a gallery artist to someone who made pots and sold them on the side of the road."

The couple started Mosey 'n Me in 1989. They design and sell cross-stitch

Personal Touches

Bye-bye, bland. Howdy, one-of-a-kind furnishings and accessories!

Take some cues from Frank and his on-air homeowner partners to create custom touches that personalize any space.

If you want your home to look like a bland furniture showroom, then move into one. Otherwise, decorate in a way that reflects you. "To me, the hardest part of decorating is to remain yourself," says Frank, who warns against succumbing to decorating peer pressure. "It takes guts to decorate in a style that's you, because chances are it's not the going thing."

In Seattle, he and his team left behind folksy-style self-portraits. In Maine, Frank went contemporary in a bachelor's bedroom, but included a little painted frog peeking out from behind the drapery. Personal touches don't have to be cute; they just need to reflect you, your lifestyle, or your interests. To discover your personal style, look through shelter magazines and books, noticing which designs you most consistently respond to. Use colors and fabrics because you like them, not because they're fashionable. Layer your room with photographs of family and friends, travel mementos, personal artwork, and any other items that have special meaning. "If you love it, you'll find a way to make it work," says Frank.

Sweet Guy: Though Frank claims to be a beer and remote kind of guy, he appreciates touches of refinement. On the road, he buys fresh flowers for his hotel room. At home, he has an antique teacup collection.

patterns and do all the peripheral activities related to that business. They regularly hold seminars throughout the country. Judy designs a special piece for the class, and they teach the class together. "It's a very animated, tell-

Frank affixes paintbrushes to the wall as part of a recent design.

all sort of psychotherapy-slash-needlework," says Frank. They both used to attend crafts conventions but had to stop because people started coming to the booth to talk about *Trading Spaces* instead of looking at the patterns.

The conventions gave Frank great exposure and some major career breaks. Someone at a

crafts show saw Frank's designs, then started publishing his work in cross-stitch books. At another crafts show, someone observed Frank doing a demonstration, and he became a guest on HGTV. Next, a TV producer who was familiar with Frank told him about a new show seeking two cohosts. Frank auditioned and got the gig, serving as cohost for *Your Home Studio*, which lasted only one season. The production company for *Your Home Studio* was Ross Productions, the same company that was developing a show based on Britain's *Changing Rooms*. Someone from Ross called Frank and told him Ross was producing a new show and needed a *Friends*-like cast of young, beautiful designers. Frank auditioned and, once

36

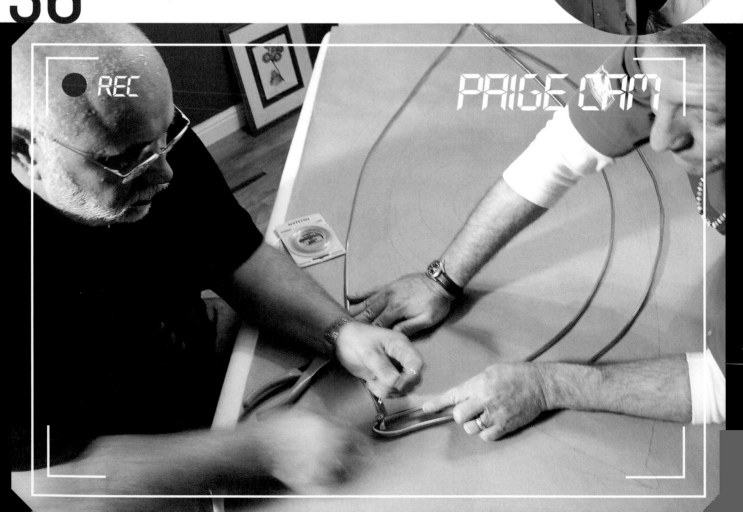

Seattle Flashback

Frank revisits an infamous episode—Seattle: 137th St.

Frank's goal of pleasing his homeowners is almost an obsession, so he took it to heart when Pam, the female homeowner on his team for the Seattle: 137th St. episode, saw her own living room (in which Doug had covered the fireplace) and ran out sobbing. Frank had worked with Pam and her husband for two days, and he sympathized entirely: "Every time I see that show, I just physically tighten up," he says. "I know how much that reaction ruined her life." That's why Frank's makeovers are often less dramatic and retain elements of the old room. "Many times people don't have the money to put it back, so you don't want to screw up their house just for a TV show," he says. "That's why I don't take down ceiling fans, because it costs to put them back up." Though the Seattle episode pains him, one part of it heartens him: The sobbing woman's husband, who also disliked the living room, said that even with the room the way it was, he wouldn't trade the two-day experience for a different outcome. "That's about the nicest thing anyone's ever said to me outside my family."

again, got the gig. "I cannot believe I'm still on the show," he says. "Let's face it—what chance does a fat, balding, sweaty, middle-aged man have on a TV show? It's like Salvador Dalí is orchestrating my life right now."

One of the more surreal aspects of Frank's job as an interior designer is that he is not trained as one and does not think of himself as one. "I think of myself as someone who draws with furniture," he says. Frank feels his lack of training and experience in this particular realm of design frees him to break rules and appreciate more diverse styles, and he finds designing rooms for *Trading Spaces* to be very easy.

For Frank, *Trading Spaces* is about the people, not the design. While other designers on the show may arrive holding detailed architectural sketches or accessories picked up in other countries, Frank usually shows up with some fabric and 10 or so paint chips. He walks around the house and seriously considers existing style, gearing the design to people's lives, not the camera. He wants the homeowners to walk in and say, "That's exactly what I would have done." He also listens carefully to his team. "What the

Frank takes a moment to contemplate his peach paint.

team wants, that's what I base my design on," he says. "I enjoy having the team do things. It's all about them."

Where Frank's life will go after the show is anybody's guess; he has no expectations except to let the show run its course. Then he'll return home and continue being Mulitdimensional Frank. Or, as Frank in his ever-so-humble way says, "At this point, my goal is just to finish the season and tile my house."

Donning a wet suit, Frank makes a splash—as well as some new aquatic friends—at the SeaWorld dolphin exhibit while taping B-roll footage in San Diego.

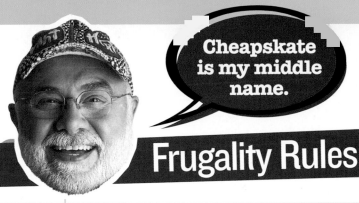

Frugality Rules

Refashion existing wood furniture: See wood pieces in a new light by giving them a fresh coat of paint or stain. Remember, paint or stain real wood pieces only; avoid painting veneers and laminates.

Frank loves the challenge of doing a room in two days for $1,000. Show after show, the designers work the system, squeezing the last drop of style out of their limited decorating dollars. Practice their tricks of the trade to create your own frugal fashion statement:

✱ **Start with a total budget in mind.** That way you stay in control, and you can figure out how much to allocate to each element in the room.

✱ **Spend your biggest chunk on a focal point.** If you draw attention to one high-quality element, your room will look impressive instead of inexpensive. Your focal point might be a fancy window treatment, an unusual armoire, or an elegant headboard.

✱ **Learn to do it yourself.** For example, wood floors that you refinish yourself will look a lot better than bland wall-to-wall carpet. Look for do-it-yourself classes through fabric stores (to learn home sewing), community colleges (to study upholstery and basic woodworking), and home centers (for decorative painting and flooring installation techniques).

✱ **Decorate over time.** *Trading Spaces* does a room in two days, but you can take your time. Know the look you're aiming for in your room, familiarize yourself with all available retail resources, and only buy when you see a deal.

✱ **Barter your skills.** If you know how to sew and your friend likes to paint, trade projects for the weekend. Or have a handy woodworker build some bookshelves in return for a week of home-cooked meals.

✱ **Buy mis-tinted paint.** Every home center has a pile of custom-tinted paints that didn't match the color some other customer envisioned. You can get a good deal on these mis-tints; some high-quality brands go for $2 per gallon. Adjust the color by mixing gallons in a large plastic pail or by adding artist's pigments to the can. Whether you're considering mis-tints or off-the-shelf paint, Frank warns against scrimping; always buy the best paint you can afford, because better coverage and greater durability offer the best value over time.

✱ **Get fabric for less.** Almost every city has a discount fabric store; find the one in your area and look for others wherever you travel. (The designers on the show regularly buy upholstery fabrics for about $7 per yard.) Also visit local upholsterers and drapery workrooms and ask to see remnants (leftovers from old jobs). Sometimes you'll find a piece that's exactly the right size for covering a chair or ottoman or creating pillows or a simple valance.

Dress up cheap fabric: Use a small amount of an expensive trim or embellishment to make plain fabrics look pretty. For example, use beaded trim to edge a muslin valance or add decorative nailhead trim to outline a polyester velvet chair.

> **My goal on the show is to create a room that can be lived in. I can't, in good conscience, leave a home knowing that I have left the homeowners with a theater set.**

Laurie Hickson Smith has always fit the profile of a fiery, determined redhead, and those characteristics came to the forefront during Spring 2000. Laurie found herself in a mental wrestling match: Personally, life was great, as she had married Brad, the love of her life the previous fall. Professionally, she enjoyed practicing interior design; however, a passion for performing kept pulling at her heartstrings. Although she loved their home in Jackson, Mississippi, it was far from the bright lights of Broadway to which she also was drawn. What she didn't know then was that *Trading Spaces* was about to come into her life—and enable her to have the best of both worlds. Laurie had graduated from the New York School of Interior Design the previous fall, while nurturing her acting ambition by taking night classes at New York's School for Film and Television. As she often

laurie hickson smith

Sophistication with a dash of Southern sass: Laurie Hickson Smith is the belle of the decorating ball wherever the *Trading Spaces* cast and crew travel.

Confessions of a Style Mixmaster

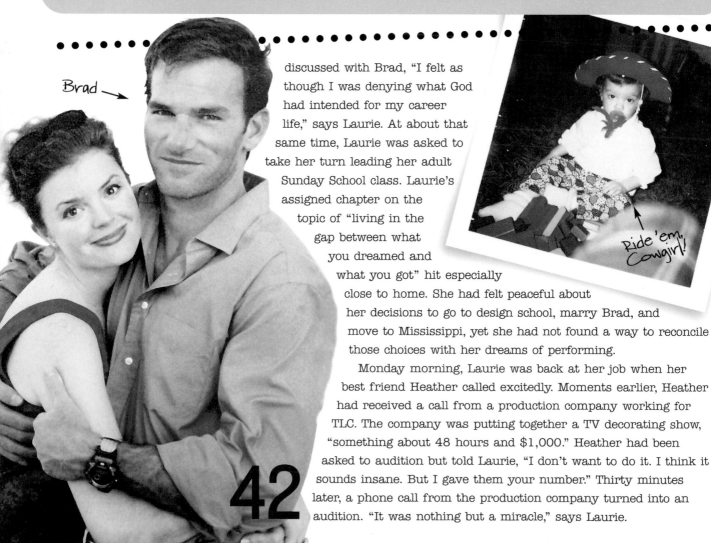

"I call myself a contemporary classic," says Laurie, whose rooms are never completely traditional or totally modern, but always a mix of the two styles. She loves antique furniture and formal arrangements, but she's also drawn to abstract contemporary art and of-the-moment color schemes. Her own taupe and butter-color living room is filled with antique French furniture, floor-to-ceiling draperies, and a giant sunburst mirror, but next to her traditional sofa stand sleek midcentury Barcelona stools with chrome bases. Whatever objects or colors Laurie uses, her rooms strictly conform to the principles of classicism—the proper scale of items in relation to the human body and the proper proportion of objects in relation to each other. Laurie finds that an emphasis on symmetry and geometry—essential to classicism—translates equally well to traditional and modern design; this is her key to blending disparate items into a cohesive decorating scheme. For example, Laurie's master bedroom design for the Jackson: Golden Pond bedroom on page 49 is equal parts fresh and formal. The color scheme of icy aqua, cream, and chocolate, combined with mahogany wood tones, practically defines modern style today. Also modern is the grid-pattern headboard, which is softened by a traditional damask bedspread and plaid pillow shams. On either side of the bed, carved and bronzed candlestick lamp bases look sleeker with white drum shades. On the fireplace wall, a classic white wood mantel is topped with a bronzed, molded wood frame containing a sleek grid of mirror tiles. Flanking the fireplace are bookcases that repeat the grid motif, but crown molding links them to the fireplace. In front of the fireplace, old English caneback chairs are re-covered to fit the new color scheme. "It's a fine line to walk between two styles," says Laurie. But the results are well worth the effort.

Brad →

discussed with Brad, "I felt as though I was denying what God had intended for my career life," says Laurie. At about that same time, Laurie was asked to take her turn leading her adult Sunday School class. Laurie's assigned chapter on the topic of "living in the gap between what you dreamed and what you got" hit especially close to home. She had felt peaceful about her decisions to go to design school, marry Brad, and move to Mississippi, yet she had not found a way to reconcile those choices with her dreams of performing.

Ride 'em, Cowgirl!

Monday morning, Laurie was back at her job when her best friend Heather called excitedly. Moments earlier, Heather had received a call from a production company working for TLC. The company was putting together a TV decorating show, "something about 48 hours and $1,000." Heather had been asked to audition but told Laurie, "I don't want to do it. I think it sounds insane. But I gave them your number." Thirty minutes later, a phone call from the production company turned into an audition. "It was nothing but a miracle," says Laurie.

> ## "I'll never forget Frank turning to me and saying, 'Laurie, get over it. It's only going to last three weeks; then it'll be over. No one will ever watch this show.'

Dad Mom Bro Laurie

Within three weeks of that phone call, Laurie flew to Knoxville, Tennessee, joining designer Frank Bielec to shoot the premiere episode of *Trading Spaces*. Chaos reigned. Back then, during the earliest episodes, the designers didn't get pictures and room specifications beforehand. Laurie and Frank had to fly in, look at the rooms, make a plan, shop for all the supplies in an unfamiliar city, and start shooting the next day. As she and Frank drove around Knoxville searching out stores, she anxiously asked him, "Frank, what are we going to do?" Laurie recalls, "I'll never forget him turning to me and saying,

'Laurie, get over it. It's only going to last three weeks; then it'll be over. No one will ever watch this show.'"

Three years later, the show qualifies for cult status. "I certainly didn't think I'd have 6-year-olds running up to me asking for my autograph," says Laurie, who is pleased by the recognition of fans and the popularity of the show. "Who thought 6-year-olds would be interested in interior design?"

Though Laurie's room makeovers aren't as shocking as some of the other designers' work, Laurie does have strong opinions about what interior design should be.

"My goal on the show is to create a room that can be lived in," says Laurie. "I can't, in good conscience, leave a home knowing that I have left the

Gibson Mom

Landscape Painter: At a Colorado wilderness camp, 14-year-old Laurie's creative side could not be suppressed. While performing a 36-hour "solo" in which she was dropped off in the woods to survive alone without food or water, Laurie made it through the night by sleeping under a boulder. She spent the following day soaking up the sun and gathering berries to make paint so she could paint in her journal.

homeowners with a theater set," she says. Laurie believes home should be a place of solace, an escape from a crazy outside world, so her designs tend to be tailored, clean, and orderly.

However, clean design doesn't mean staid. With each makeover, Laurie aims to create a dynamic relationship between modern and traditional furnishings and design elements. For example, she has combined contemporary tricolor stripes painted horizontally around a room with traditional floor-to-ceiling French pleat draperies; a modern, gridlike upholstered headboard with damask and plaid bedding; Mondrian-inspired artwork and conduit-pipe shelving with crewelwork pillows.

> **Laurie carefully regards her wall color selection.**

"I like to walk the fine line between the classic and contemporary and marry them in my rooms," Laurie says.

No matter how clean Laurie's design, the television show's avid viewers know that some

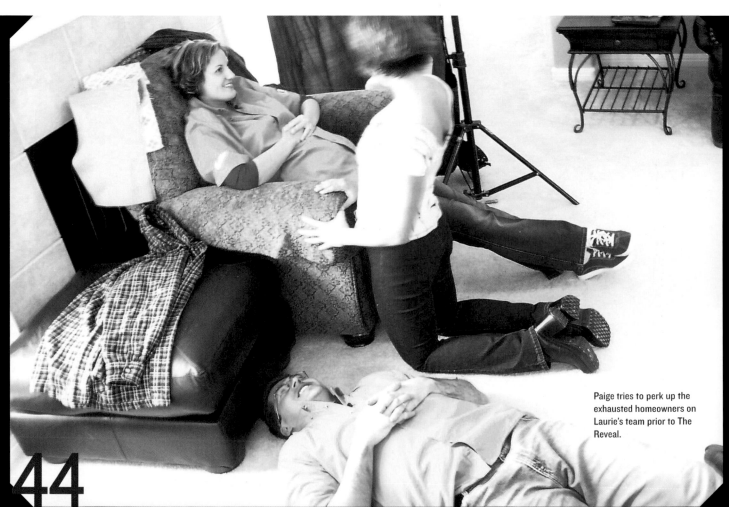

Paige tries to perk up the exhausted homeowners on Laurie's team prior to The Reveal.

Focal Point Fabrics

The Material Girl recounts some cloth encounters of the thrilling kind...

A bona fide fabric junkie, Laurie explains how to pump up any room transformation with carefully selected threads.

A fabulous fabric find is at the heart of almost every one of Laurie's rooms. Frequently, a mere smidgen of fabric will inspire the concept for an entire design. "I look to the fabric to make an artistic statement in the room," says Laurie. To that end, she looks for unusual focal point fabrics that have interesting patterns and bold color combinations. She then adds solids or more standard fabric patterns as complements. One of her favorite fabrics is silk, which she likes for its body and the way it catches light. When designing for families with children, she opts for more durable material, such as chenille, linen, velvet, and cottons with fun prints.

Laurie says anyone can build a room around a fabric. "Find a fabric you truly love, even if it ends up being a pillow that costs $100 per yard," she says, adding that the best choice is something "that has a color combination that just sings." This was her approach when she designed a modern masculine office, which she furnished with terra-cotta-color walls and conduit-pipe shelving. She chose a graphic crewelwork containing touches of black as the focal point.

Fabulous fabric won't bust your budget if you use it strategically. Laurie insists that even small amounts can become the centerpiece of a room. If you like a very expensive fabric, use it as a center pillow on the sofa or as a cover for an ottoman or for a bench in front of the fireplace. Yards of less expensive fabric can then be used for larger projects—draperies or sofa upholstery, for instance. In the modern masculine office, the crewelwork stands out from everything else in the room, yet it's used on only one sofa pillow and three floor pillows.

fabulous fabric will be involved. If Laurie busts a budget, it's usually fabric that puts her over. While most of the other designers spend $5 to $7 a yard for their fabrics, the crewelwork for Laurie's pillows cost $45 a yard—on sale.

Part of watching any Laurie episode is anticipating at which point during the two days she's going to have an, albeit well-mannered, stress attack. Now that the television production is a little more organized and Laurie has dozens of episodes under her belt, you'd think the perfectionist would be able to relax. You may have noticed that Season 2 documents her pregnancy, and in Season 3 baby Gibson debuts, making Laurie the

only cast member with a young child.

She has good reason to be stressed. For starters, during Laurie's first episodes after her maternity leave, Gibson was on the set (with the care of a nanny), and Laurie was nursing. By Day 2, Laurie realized that her attempts at discretion were futile. At one point, she was nursing Gibson on a homeowner's living room sofa, surrounded by no less than nine cast and crew members.

For stressor number 2, they were shooting in her

Ever mindful of her budget and color palette, eagle-eyed Laurie hunts for thrifty window treatments, accessories, housewares, and more.

lauri erickson smith

Born: May 23, 1971
Raised: Houston, Texas

Adopted Hometown: Jackson, Mississippi
Dirty Little Secret: Laurie actually likes ceiling fans
and has four in her own home.

Brush with Fame: Laurie once shared a limo with
Ted Turner and Jane Fonda on the way to the
IMAX theater in Manhattan for the release party
of the Beatles video anthology that Laurie
worked on as a marketing executive.

Photographed in Austin, Texas on November 15, 2002

Goin' to the chapel: Laurie and friends celebrate Laurie and Brad's wedding day.

Art Fan: Laurie's favorite artists are 19th- and 20th-century abstract painters who focus on color. She's fond of the contemporary German painter Wolf Kahn. Of Kahn she says, "He's abstract and uses vivid, sometimes wild color. How he chooses to place colors together, many times, has inspired the color palettes for my rooms."

adopted hometown of Jackson, Mississippi, so there was the added confusion of local news crews and photographers. The homeowners who were working with Laurie happened to be longtime friends. The other homeowners, whose room she was designing, are acquaintances whom she will see again, so she couldn't help but feeling the added pressure to make sure the room was as carefully constructed as it was beautiful.

48

Adding to the stress load, producers from *The Oprah Winfrey Show* were trying to get Laurie and another show designer,

Genevieve Gorder, to make over some undisclosed rooms in an undisclosed city, with the shoot scheduled to begin the day after the Jackson shoot finished up. As she walked through the homeowners' kitchen, Laurie jokingly clutched her stomach and pitched forward.

Laurie and Vern savor a "level"-headed moment on the set.

As a child in Houston, Laurie thought her performance career would be as a dancer. At the height of her 10 years of training, she left school early every day to start dance classes at 2 p.m., continued until 10 p.m.,

Laurie's scintillating combination of plum and ruby red fabrics, set off against golden walls and window treatments, transformed this Jackson, Mississippi, bedroom from blah to beautiful.

fitting her homework in between. She also performed in school plays. When she was in sixth grade, her parents took her to visit New York City. The showbiz glamour and the abundance of cultural activity made the city a Mecca in Laurie's mind.

"I spent my whole childhood running around the house singing songs from *Annie*," she says.

Laurie's banker father and homemaker mother moved the family across the South several times during Laurie's childhood. "It forced me to fend for myself and get to know people and step into the game," she says. By the time Laurie reached ninth grade, the family had moved to El Paso, where there was no ballet company. The ever-adaptable Laurie shifted to theater, winning the city championship in the solo dramatic interpretation category that year. She spent her high school years at a large, primarily Hispanic public high school, which made her "hypersensitive and aware of how other people are feeling when they're not like everybody else," says Laurie. During the summers, she attended camp, including a serious theater camp at Phillips Academy in Andover, Massachusetts, taught by a member of the

Gibson

> "If someone had told me then that I'd be blessed enough to be on a television show with this huge following, be married to the love of my life, and be living in Jackson, Mississippi, being driven by a driver taking me to a photo shoot in SoHo—it's amazing to me.

Ready for her close-up: Laurie confers with an on-set producer and other crew members to make sure she's hitting her mark during the filming of a Jackson, Mississippi, episode.

Yale University theater department. When she went off to college at Southern Methodist University, Laurie bowed to practical advice and majored in broadcast journalism rather than dance or theater. As an ABC intern, she was on site during the siege on David Koresh's compound in Waco, Texas. "I loved telling a story in front of the camera. What I didn't love enough was hard-core news," says Laurie, who preferred reporting on the arts.

During the following years, Laurie struggled to find her place in the corporate world, trying to match her circumstances with her ambitions. She worked for a communications consulting company, coaching executives and politicians and at a marketing firm that helped launch the children's television program *Wishbone*. Then she moved to Atlanta to work for TBS, where she worked on the marketing team that launched the *Beatles Anthology* video series. She then made marketing and advertising spots for TNT Originals. "I ended up at TNT because I loved TV and film, not because I loved

51

> ❝ Saying I wanted to go to interior design school just sounded flighty. I even questioned it myself. ❞

marketing," she says.

Laurie's sudden decision to study interior design was inspired by her hope for a career that would be both creative and flexible. Although she expressed a long-time love of art and architecture, numerous European trips (including memorable visits to Spain, Morocco, Italy, and England) helped develop Laurie's appreciation of classic as well as contemporary European style. While her parents and friends were surprised by her career decision, Laurie says she fell in love with interior design and discovered she was good at it. Her new career twist finally took her to New York City and

eventually, after several more twists and turns, to her on-camera dream job on *Trading Spaces*.

During her lowest time, Laurie often viewed her life as a series of zigzags—choices and circumstances that never quite took her where she truly wanted to go. Now she looks back on her different interests, relocations, and career changes as "God's perfectly

Always a sunbeam, teenage Laurie grins and bears it.

orchestrated plan" that guided her to the job she'd always wanted: performing. "I love to be in front of the camera or in a crowd telling a story," says Laurie. "It brings me profound joy."

doug wilson

"Now, Doug, you have to know how much I love you, but there have been times when if you showed up on my doorstep, I'd have had to slam my door in your face. —**Marilyn Romani**, a Woodriver, Illinois, fan"

A tiny sign travels across America with *Trading Spaces*. It reads "Danger! Doug's Room" and inevitably wins smiles from all who enter, including a sly, satisfied grin from Douglas Wilson himself. With a will as strong as his paint colors, Doug knows what it means to be loved and feared by the homeowners who open their doors to him. And although he'd much rather be loved, for now he's content having earned his place on the edge. After all, that's where creative leaps are made.

For anxious homeowners and a television crew on a schedule, the only real danger to fear in Doug's rooms lies in those moments of not knowing what will come next. Watching his rooms evolve is proof that having a vision is not the same as having an outlined plan. Doug knows how he works best: He may confidently walk into a store for sunny yellow paint and confidently walk out with brilliant dusk orange. He can shop for eight hours without a glance at the list he thinks exists under pages of scribbled notes and drawings—but doesn't. He carries a PalmPilot, which he pulls out once in three days to use as a calculator. "It's all up here," says Doug, tapping a

Left: Doug Wilson grew up on a farm in central Illinois. Captivated by the theater at age 14, he performed in musicals in high school and college, then headed for New York City to study with the National Shakespeare Conservatory. **Above:** Skill as a self-taught handyman and carpenter snagged him a spot on *Trading Spaces*.

> **"** I hoped Doug would throw that couch. He said he might, and I secretly wished he would. But I couldn't ask him. I couldn't take the responsibility. Good thing, too, since they had to do three takes and took out a gutter on the way down. **—Larry Base,** *Trading Spaces* producer on the Berkeley: Prospect Street episode, Delta Upsilon fraternity room **"**

finger to his head when he should really be pointing to his gut.

Doug is forever faced with homeowner conflicts, but his difficulties have less to do with a lack of people skills than with the challenge of convincing others to try ideas they'd rather see someone else (namely, the designer) work out first. "Can't always have time to practice," jokes Doug, who wants his team to face the winds of change with all the joy of a puppy sticking its head out the window of a moving car. Some of his designs are extreme:

converting a bedroom into a Pullman car or installing stadium seating in a family room used for sleepovers. Even in a more conventional room—for example, "A Pretty Room by Doug" (Season 2, Houston: Appalachian Trail)—the element of the unknown can make Doug's design feel risky to the average homeowner. As a Washington, D.C., homeowner quipped back to him, "Wish you spent as much time planning this as you did on your hair this morning."

Doug Puppet

Humor is what makes the going easy. Doug encourages it. He's the only designer to literally throw out existing furniture—three stories down through

56

SP
0:28:40:21
34min

Homeowner Update

Indiana: River Valley Drive

Doug's "Back to Brazil" room also brought him back to the drawing board. Hours slipped away due to the challenges of television, including waiting for a burned-out lightbulb to be replaced and a noisy washing machine to finish its cycle. In the meantime, Doug abandoned his original complex stencil pattern in favor of a mum-stripe explosion that his team might be able to complete in time. The result? "Hideous!" exclaims Doug.

Although Doug counts this room as his biggest disappointment, Indiana homeowners Brad and Dana Loftus remain grateful they opened their doors to him. They love the sleek, oversize fireplace surround, the slipcovers, the shuttered doors, and the furniture arrangement. "The light fixture came down, and yeah, we painted over the flowers with the original wall color," says Brad, "but we used a gloss finish versus flat to keep the stripes. It's a little funky, something we wouldn't have done before. Our home is definitely the better for having had Doug come in to disturb it all."

That's pretty forgiving, considering that Doug used the Loftuses' steak knife to cut his toenails. As for that triptych painting of a large hairy foot? Neighbor Craig Vermeulen promises to paint Brad and Dana something different; he's contemplating a still life with a wine bottle. They're saving the wall space. Doug concludes, "That's the whole point, isn't it? One friend making art for another?"

the window of a fraternity house attic. He plays the *Trading Spaces* diva for sport, joking about coffee breaks (although he never actually takes them) or coolly referring to a Maine homeowner as "you, helper number two."

When a Quakertown woman asked for a small cup of paint to avoid climbing up and down a ladder, Doug returned with the homeowner's best china teacup overflowing with chocolate brown paint. "Totally washable," he still insists.

On a good day, Doug's infectious brand of edgy fun can push his team to new creative heights. The designer most likely to make crafts time rowdy, he has nudged some otherwise good neighbors into offering up risqué personalized artwork: enlarged views of hairy feet or a private photo of a homeowner. "I didn't go searching through her drawers like you think," he says in his own defense. "Her neighbor told me about that photo and exactly where to find it." On other days, Doug's methods can have the opposite effect, inciting rebellion by the homeowners or, in one D.C.-area neighborhood, by the designer himself, who walked out on his team to cool down.

Just remember who's the designer here!

DANGER

DOUG'S ROOM

7

He's arrogant, some fans of the show claim. Lazy, say others. "That's the one remark I can't stand to hear. It's just not true," says Doug's mom, who knows darn well when her son is lounging in a lawn chair and sipping tea for laughs. It seems Doug's "bad boy" image is a stretch from the strapping young farm boy who made good grades while keeping up on his chores, theatrical and choir

His father, however, knew how to reinvent a space. He looked at the expanse of wood plank floors in the high-ceilinged loft of the family's barn and saw a new basketball court for his boys. Then, long before Kevin Costner got the idea in *Field of Dreams,* Doug's dad mowed down a patch of land to

Long before his infamous "Going Ballistic" room, Doug had an affinity for orbs.

> " Sure, I'd let him make over a room in our house...though I don't know what his dad would say. And you know our Doug doesn't like to do things halfway. —Doug's mom "

rehearsals, and his duties as district student council president.

Doug grew up baling hay and walking the rows of beans on his family's century-old farm in central Illinois. The fourth of five brothers, he was more victim than bully. Any early decorating tendencies he had were put on hold while he roomed with the brothers and a unanimously agreed-upon poster of Farrah Fawcett. "We never painted, but we did draw a line down the room to map out our turf," remembers Doug.

build a major-league-size baseball field surrounded by miles of corn and big open sky.

Sports meant everything in rural Illinois, and Doug played his share—football, basketball, baseball, and track and field. But the same year he batted .500 (he was at bat only 18 times and got 9 hits), his outlook changed forever.

His mom took him along to a community playhouse production of *Oklahoma!* Afterward, she says, "He looked right up at the stage and said, 'I'm going to be up there next year.

Above: Doug played Danny Zuko in *Grease.* **Right:** Doug as Frank Butler in *Annie Get Your Gun* at the University of Illinois. Broadway beckoned, and Doug quit college to organize his own variety show. Then he headed East to study with the National Shakespeare Conservatory.

58

Doug and his mom.

I can sing better than that boy.'" Doug was right. Next year he was in the spotlight, yodeling the "Lonely Goatherd" solo as Friedrich, the eldest boy in *The Sound of Music*. Breaking his school's high jump record still ranked high on Doug's list of accomplishments, but even that took second fiddle to playing a vagrant in *Li'l Abner*.

Many musicals later, Doug enrolled at the University of Illinois, where he starred in college and professional productions, including *Annie Get Your Gun* and *Grease*. He also joined a fraternity, where he came up with the hip soundproofing solution of upholstering his walls, floors, and ceiling in low-pile navy blue carpet. ("If I saw it in a house today, that carpet would have to go," he says.) But campus life

From Runway to His Way Doug's Evolving Fashion Sense

Black shirt, black pants, black knit cap	Doug sported this little burglar suit to steal the show with his design for a Deco-inspired movie theater inside a Portland family room. Dressed head to toe in black, he also blacked out the room's windows. Some fans raved how Doug's theater scheme made creative use of a too-dark space, converted from the old garage. Others, however, found him suitably dressed for crimes against architecture.	
Black leather pants	These pants are now synonymous with Doug's groovy, á la Austin Powers design for a Berkeley fraternity house, where the rock 'n' roll-clad designer smashed furniture instead of a guitar. But fans first saw Doug strut leather in the Los Angeles: Willoughby Avenue episode, where his design was as slick as his new pants: a trippy wall stencil shaped like abstract TV sets and a U-shape platform couch lit at the base to glow in the dark.	
Flip-flops	Doug wears flip-flops for a more casual mood, such as his "Back to Brazil" design. Such simple footwear is proof that the diva designer really can kick back and lay low on budget too. Familiar with pricier, trendier versions in New York storefronts, Doug opted to purchase his flip-flops at a discount store while shopping for a *Trading Spaces* room. All he had to do was rub out the Baywatch insignia on the arch of each shoe.	
Changing hair styles	His hair is proof that this designer never stops trying. Having modeled styles ranging from New Wave curls to a Fonzarelli comb-back, Doug has learned that not all hair plays on camera. "It took me years to get a good cut," he laughs. "I used to get a lot of frizz, so I'd put in some mousse. Then I'd see myself on TV and say, 'Oh, look at Mr. Slick.'"	
Jeans and wool coat	A Midwestern plains boy at heart, Doug is at home in comfortable jeans and the kind of warm wool coat worn on weekend trips to the country. No wonder he packed an outfit similar to this in his suitcase before getting back to his roots with an "Autumn Harvest" design, which blended the colors of sunsets and wheat in an Indiana bedroom.	

doug wilson

Born: November 4, 1964
Raised: Central Illinois
Adopted Hometown: New York City
Backup Career Skills: Good with a squeegee and power drill
Most Heartwarming Apology: "I love you; do you still love me?"
Photographed outside Austin, Texas on November 17, 2002

couldn't compete with the call of Broadway. Intent on busting out to the Big Apple, Doug cut short his college career and assembled his own benefit variety show. *The Road to New York* included a magic act and ended with a stirring

Being handy with a jigsaw looks good on the resume.

performance of Barbra Streisand's "People," sung by the producer himself. The show raised $3,000 in ticket sales (a hefty sum in 1986), and enjoyed a three-night run at the same local theater where Doug launched his acting career.

Once in New York, Doug chose a decidedly unavant-garde route, opting for classical training at the now-

defunct National Shakespeare Conservatory. Low on funds but high on drive, he worked his way up, then down, as a window washer, dangling from the sides of skyscrapers 40 stories above the street. Over the years he found steady work performing in theater outreach plays for troubled teens and brought home larger paychecks as a handyman and later, a carpenter, doing general home repairs.

Doug arrived in town with few trade skills, but that was no obstacle. To start with, he called home to the farm and asked Dad how to use certain tools, or he went to the library and checked out a book. He managed well, discovered new talents, and eventually

REC   PAIGE CAM

62

Doug added a chair rail and an upholstered wainscot to offset the dauntingly high ceiling and bring the focus down to the bed. Orange paint on the walls above the chair rail warms the space. Doug and the neighbors stitched ordinary white cotton duck into a bedspread, pillow shams, and a slipcover. Embroidery-inspired cross stitches and running stitches accent the expanses of white with a touch of color.

At Home with Doug

Early indications of the designer within: in college, Doug upholstered the walls, ceiling, and floor of his dorm room with navy blue carpet.

Past

A foursquare Victorian farmhouse with deep porches and practical, sweepable wall paneling.

Present

A perpetually unfinished New York City apartment with primer white walls, bare lightbulbs, and a stack of decorating magazines piled high on a stove that he never uses.

Future

Says Doug, "I could live comfortably in the bedroom I did for those Katona, New York, lawyers, but all I really want is a small shingled cottage by the ocean."

landed on the uptown-society list of most-sought-after tradespeople. Never afraid to tackle something new, Doug raised the eyebrows of one Park Avenue client by accidentally leaving behind a well-thumbed copy of a popular guide to home repair. "She said she wasn't sure if she should be grateful I was using the book or not," he laughs.

Doug enjoyed a reputation for his outstanding detail work and, believe it or not, for his accommodating manner. Slowly, he built a boutique business specializing in elaborate decorative paint finishes. (The subtleties of his wall treatments might take up to a full week to complete.) He worked steadily for decorating legends Albert Hadley and Alexa Hampton, whose influences, like

Warned that the neighbors were practical jokers, Doug decided to make a preemptive strike and pulled his own joke on them. The neighbor retaliated by swiping him with a roller filled with green paint.

64

Above: During the shooting of B-roll footage on a dairy farm in Indiana (to open and close the show), Doug jumped on the tractor and started driving it—it was just like one he used to drive as a kid.

After the first coat of bright orange paint went up in an Indiana bedroom, the once-doubting neighbor began to come around. "It's funky," he said. "Shut up," said Doug, looking back at the orange. "Wrong word. It's *autumnal.*"

Doug's Shakespearean training, are a sign of the classicism lurking inside every one of Doug's downtown designs. Says Hampton, "He has an extensive knowledge of styles you don't see on the show, and, not to ruin his image, he's really just wonderful to work with. Of course, I have no idea what *Trading Spaces* could bring about, but in our line of work, he absolutely likes to make people happy and would never dig in his heels like that and scream 'No!'"

From Barbara Walters's dressing room to the oxblood walls of Brooke Astor's library, from the details of New York Mayor Michael

Bloomberg's townhouse to the halls of elite design showhouses, Doug has experimented with materials as diverse as crayons, convex mirrors, and tinted plaster. His rooms received write-ups in the *New York Times* as well as a bit in *House and Garden*, which quoted Doug as an expert on color and reproduced his preferred palette—one ranging from bubble

> **Doug tours the neighborhood with a homeowner's father before taping.**

gum pink and fiery reds to royal blues and brilliant purples. The accompanying photo showed Doug in a chartreuse shirt (not far from the color of his later, glow-in-the-dark Delta Upsilon chapter room) against a sunburst yellow background. The write-up caught the

65

New swing-arm lamps mounted through the padded headboard plug into a wall socket—no rewiring required. Cedar shelves are also attached to the wall to provide handy space for books.

66

after

For "Most Effective Addition of Architecture," the winner is: Doug's all-white overmantel, with white-painted mirror frame. Kudos also go to slipcovers and painted furniture for supporting roles.

before

Below: "Working with power tools is nothing new for us farm boys," says Doug. He and his team create the "Back to Brazil" room, which was inspired by a recent trip to Brazil and featured stripes of abstract flowers—not his favorite room, he admits.

attention of *Trading Spaces* producers. Snapping back to an auditioning carpenter, "Who's the designer here?" secured him the job.

Doug's current efforts are focused on decorating, but the theatrical showman is not lost. Whether he's working with silk, cowhide, windsails, or chintz, he gives every one of his rooms a title, and a few select decorative elements get starring roles. In Doug's mind, other details matter less and can change with time and budget. But homeowners who balk at the focal point of his design are, in effect, trying to recast his show; that's how he sees it. Says Doug, "I can take it if that's what the neighbors want for their friends—if that's how they think their friends should be living, versus what they know for sure their friends will like. But then, if they could see all the possibilities they'd be open to, I wouldn't be there. Would I?"

Name Game
For two seasons Doug was the only designer to title his rooms. Some are descriptive, others just wordplay.

"Cocteau Country"

Otherwise known as French Country style, but with Doug's customary twist. The French author and filmmaker Jean Cocteau filled his home with found objects and plaster casts. The inside joke? Some of Cocteau's plaster casts reproduced certain body parts. Doug, however, stuck to casting a pitchfork pilfered from the homeowner's barn. But that didn't work out. So Doug improvised and spray painted his found objects white.

"A Pretty Room"

The italics are all important, as demonstrated in person by Doug with a slightly angelic tilt of the head. Meanwhile the room's gentle sky blues, grays, and whites take inspiration from the clouds. Really, Doug's a nice guy, this room seems to say. His mother agrees, adding, "He dedicated his pretty blue room to me. It's my favorite. I'm still waiting for the duvet cover he promised to make me from the leftover fabric."

"Suburban Safari"

A Pennsylvania couple dreamed of a bedroom that might take them on the honeymoon they never had. Doug took their thatched-hut theme into the wild with a jungle motif of all-over safari stripes. Just what was he hunting with those walls? Believe it or not, subtlety. The homeowners thought they were done after a long day of painting brown zebra stripes, but Doug insisted they refine the effect with layers of washes.

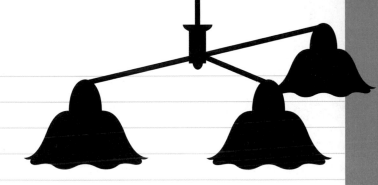

> **"** I've told Hildi this—I thought she might be a problem. She is very reserved on-camera and stoic. Once you get to know her, she's one of the funniest people off-camera I've ever met in my life. She's hysterical. **"** —**Edward Walker,** fellow *Trading Spaces* designer

Hildi Santo Tomás is the kind of person meek souls might find intimidating. One evening, inside one of the better restaurants in Jackson, Mississippi, murky light envelops the designer as she shifts comfortably sideways in a sizable black booth. Having finished Designer Chat only minutes earlier, she is decked out in a black, figure-skimming dress, diamond cross necklace, and her signature hair flip. She orders her filet mignon raw, changes the side dish to something she likes better, and when her meat arrives says, "Oh, look, it is perfect. It looks cold."

Approaching her meal with gusto, she clears her plate in between swallows of Pinot Noir. If she's tired, it doesn't show. She talks loud, she talks quickly, and her hands fly. When asked about herself, she peppers the conversation with comments such as "There is no limit to my mind—there is no fear," "I have the eye of the tiger," and "I have ideas and I am not afraid to execute them." Her voice is throaty, and when she reverts to Spanish to answer her mother's call on her cell phone, her voice is throatier still. Hildi's confidence and fearlessness could easily be off-putting; instead, they're alluring. After people who have only seen her on TV meet Hildi in person,

hildi santo tomás

Opposite and above: Hildi Santo Tomás, *Trading Spaces'* most fearless designer, and faithful companion Pluto beneath the Eiffel Tower in Hildi's adopted home, Paris.

The Reveal is the climax for the other designers who expectantly stare at a monitor in an adjacent room while the homeowners pass judgment on the new design. Hildi often skips this part because, in her mind, her work is done. She already knows the room is fabulous.

they regularly report back that they like her so much more than they thought they would. As she engages a young waiter in small talk, he is grinning and leaning in, pleased to be basking in Hildi-ness. On the set, Hildi's coworkers are drawn to her. The male crew members noticeably light up when her attention lands on them. Then they steal sideways glances of her figure as she walks away with a sweet scent of perfume trailing behind her. Paige considers her a woman any girl could look up

to, adding, "She's a lady with every fiber of her being."

To make time for dinner and an interview, Hildi left the set before the homeowner Reveal—the climax for the other designers who expectantly stare at a monitor in an adjacent room while the homeowners pass judgment on the new design. Hildi often skips this part because, in her mind, her work is done. She already knows the room is fabulous. Whether the homeowner likes it is of little concern to Hildi. More than 5 million people watch each episode of the

Left: Hildi's take on the signature Tiffany & Co. blue box. The white graffiti scrawls represent white ribbons. **Above:** From one homeowner to another...

Well Heeled — Designer footwear keeps this feisty designer on her toes.

Whereas Genevieve and Doug may love baring their soles, the always perfectly accessorized Hildi is renowned for having the most fashionable footwear on the show. Who can forget the male homeowner who went toe-to-toe with her in a pair of high-heel, open-toe sandals?

The question is, how does Hildi maneuver around all those messy paint trays and not get splatters on her Manolos? "Heels ground me. If you watch the shows where I am wearing flats, I am not moving," she says. "I have always worn heels. I think it is a Latin thing."

Top: Shopping for paint and copper pipe—and cruising the aisles.
Bottom: Hildi loves having a hand in the creation of the projects in a room, especially if they are going to show up on-camera.

show—any number of them may love the room.

Some viewers may be surprised to learn that off-camera Hildi's self-possession is interlaced with warmth, thoughtfulness, and humor. During a crew dinner hosted by Laurie's parents in their home, Hildi is engaging and complimentary. Paige acknowledges that Hildi has an "abrasive quality of confidence" and admits that Hildi is "severe in a way." Of everyone in the cast, Paige notes, "She's the most in touch with people's feelings—she's the most sensitive." Paige would know: She was once caring for her uncle while her aunt was in the hospital, and of all the people in her life, Hildi was the only person who called to check up on Paige. To this day, Hildi still inquires about Paige's aunt.

On-camera, however, Hildi is not being paid to give out warm fuzzies.

"I am not here to be a movie star," she says. "I am here to change this room." On TV, Hildi comes across as sternly directive and unwavering. She confronted one uncooperative homeowner by saying, "Everyone in America knows I can rip up that carpet if I want to." Hildi knows that some viewers think she's a witch. "I could not care less. I am not," she says. "I think I am fun." The show is her job, and she's very

As a wallpaper substitute, 5,000 wine labels were applied to the walls.

focused on that job; she doesn't have time to worry about her on-the-air image.

Hildi is high-energy. During the course of six days of filming, she was observed resting only once, and that was at midnight, four hours before she had to leave for the airport. While doing her rooms, she works quickly and tries to do most tasks herself, especially if they're

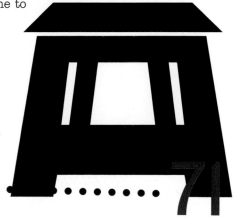

Puppy Love

Etienne may be Hildi's Prince Charming, but meet Pluto, her "other man."

Hildi's Pluto collection →

Anyone who thinks Hildi is cold should see her lavish attention on her dog. "Everybody thinks that I think that he is a real person, which I do," says Hildi of Pluto, a cinnamon-color Lab. She got him while she was living in Atlanta; he was 6 weeks old. "Yeah, Etienne is my soulmate and all that stuff," she says, but she's devoted to the dog: "Pluto is my heir, my life source, my soul."

During a phone call, Hildi explains that she and Etienne just returned home to Paris and found that their car had been stolen and the keys to their other car were in the stolen car. At the same time, Pluto, back from an extended romp in the country, has ear mites. "I could not care less about the car," says Hildi. "All I care about is that he is OK."

> "Hildi has so much energy, a real multitasker by far. She'll be doing seventeen things as she's asking you for something and pulling them all off. She comes up with the wildest ideas, and when other say it can't be done, she says, 'I will find a way.' —**Amy Wynn,** *Trading Spaces* carpenter

projects that will show up on-camera. "I do want complete control of my room," says the self-proclaimed perfectionist.

Whether she is nurturing coworkers off-camera or imposing her will on-camera, Hildi has a big personality that is quite at home with living large. In the United States, she has a townhouse in Atlanta where she lived for several years and an apartment in Miami that she shares with her sister. Her primary residence is a Paris apartment adjacent to the monument Les Invalides, where she was married in June 2002 at the age of 41. She married a Frenchman, Etienne, which in France makes her Madame Etienne Fougeron. Through Etienne's family the couple has two country houses. One is a more casual château used for weekend hunting

¡Te amo, Mamacita Hildi!

Pluto →

(Etienne is an esteemed falconer); the other is a more elegant structure, surrounded by formal gardens and a forest, and it is used primarily during holidays. Far from downplaying her lifestyle so that people won't think she's pretentious, Hildi revels in her life and the opportunities she's been given. While designing a red toile bedroom, she is eager to point out that the toile and velvet are from Paris and that the bird picture is from London. She plucked the long feathers from a pheasant she hunted herself in Belgium and carried them back to the States in her golf bag. She's not showing off; she merely wants to share the bounty of her travels. She recognizes that these items are uncommon and believes that novelty, or distinction, makes good design.

As a child, Hildi was unique in her

environment. Her parents and older sister fled Fidel Castro's Cuba in 1960, settling in Raleigh, North Carolina, where Hildi and her younger sister were born. A Cuban in Raleigh in the '60s was an uncommon sight, but Hildi liked that. She was the only one among her friends who had her ears pierced, the only one who spoke Spanish. "I would rather be different," she says. Having such a dramatic family history has shaped her in many ways. Three overarching things guided her upbringing: First, Hildi is Cuban. "We were brought up to be very Latin, Spanish, Cuban," she says. "That is how I perceive myself." Her family has never spoken English to each other. "We happened to be in Raleigh, but we lived in our own little world," she says. Being Hispanic is so close to Hildi's heart that it's always been her dream to have a husband who could speak Spanish with her. She got her wish. Etienne is French, but his mother spent much time in Spain, so he learned Spanish too; thus, Spanish is the couple's common language. The clincher: World traveler Etienne has visited Hildi's homeland 10 times on various hunting excursions.

Secondly, Hildi is American. "This is the land of opportunity, the land of freedom. That is why we came here," she says. Her family is proud to live in the

Wedding Day

Hotel des Invalides

Etienne

73

United States. Cuba's upheaval crystallized the family's political ideals ("To us, Castro is a cancer," she says) and motivated them to make a difference in their new country. Her family remains actively involved in politics today.

Finally, people matter most to Hildi. In Cuba, her family was well-to-do. Her father was a businessman who owned insurance agencies and car dealerships. When her parents fled Cuba, however, they were reduced to hiding dollar bills in a tube of toothpaste and a container of talcum powder. In Raleigh, her father had to start over. He got his insurance license and opened an agency. Says Hildi of her childhood, "We did not grow up with a lot of material things." But she didn't mind: "The cars, the homes, the jewelry—none of that stuff mattered," she says. "The most

Bathing beauties

Hildi's Infamous Rooms in Your Style

Arguably the biggest risk taker on the show, Hildi does a lot of love 'em or hate 'em rooms. She's not expecting you to copy her design; she'd rather inspire you to adapt her designs in your own way, with different colors, different items, and in different rooms.

Hildi's Way... Done Your Way...

Silk Flower Bathroom

Covering a wall with any item en masse makes a bold statement. In a kitchen or butler's pantry, use wine labels, seed packets, recipes, plates, or nice pots and pans. In a kid's room or family room, cover one wall in vinyl records or CDs. Line a closet wall with a T-shirt collection.

Quadrant Living Room

The key is continuity—making everything in the violet corners violet and everything in the gray corners gray. If you want to divide walls in the middle as Hildi did, you might choose, say, a boy's bedroom and primary colors. Instead of dividing walls, paint each of the four walls a different color, carrying each hue onto the ceiling so that triangle points of color come together at the ceiling center.

Straw Walls Living Room

This is Hildi's idea of grass-cloth wallcovering on a meager budget and tight schedule. Use real grass cloth if you can; in a dining room or foyer, it can add elegant texture. Even if you can't afford wallcovering, enhance walls with other textural elements, such as bamboo blinds, woven matting, or decorative paper. Achieve elegance by pairing textured walls with lined silk curtains and a sisal rug.

Circus Tent Family Room

Hildi's contrasting colors make this room a shocker, but wouldn't a tented baby's room look oh-so-sweet in a single shade of pastel tulle? Use a tone-on-tone silk to turn a dining room into a jewel box or use outdoor fabrics to define a patio or porch room. The tent technique lets you divide space without building walls—a definite advantage for budget-conscious do-it-yourselfers.

important thing was that our family could leave." Having her family healthy and together means more to her than being rich. And her awareness of her family's background—her knowledge that things really could be worse—makes Hildi almost unflappable in the face of day-to-day problems. She's an intense person, but she doesn't stress. "Even on *Trading Spaces*, when something goes bad, there is always a way to fix it."

Louvre

Although her family history and cultural background influence her life, Hildi doesn't dwell on the past, particularly past experiences or accomplishments. "I do not ever look back," she says. She doesn't look forward either. She is always in the moment. Any progress she has made has happened without her planning it. "I am not a goal-oriented person," she says. "I do not live my life with many expectations."

Hildi doesn't volunteer a lot of information about herself but will answer direct questions. Hildi discloses that she was an artistic and project-oriented child but that she never

Left and above: Hildi and Pluto exploring the streets of Paris. **Below:** Hildi visits with friends in a Parisian cafe.

hildi santo tomás

Born: April 4, 1961
Raised: Raleigh, North Carolina
Adopted Hometown: Paris, France
Favorite Saying: "Tell me, and I forget, teach me, and I may remember, involve me, and I will learn."—Benjamin Franklin
Annoying Habit: "I am very neat and organized. I am sure that would really annoy a lot of people. I do make lists—major lists."
For Fun: Painting, drawing, and cooking—"Food and knives, they are like paint and brushes to me."
Photographed in Paris, France on November 22, 2002

studied art or design formally, because being creative was something she liked to do on her own. And even though creative design is now her career, she has an unconventional view of

Family focus: Hildi with her sisters, above, and niece, right

what that means: "It is my freedom; it is my yoga; it is my relaxation," she says.

Though she's artistic, she has an equal facility for numbers. "I love math and business. I have a calculator brain," she says. "Whether it is upholstering or painting a room, I can scan and multiply

and know how much yardage I need in a minute." At the University of North Carolina, Chapel Hill, she started out premed, then switched to industrial relations (people management) and economics. She didn't think too hard about her course of study or what she would do with it. After college, she moved to D.C. and, like her older sister before her and younger

sister after her, became a stockbroker and financial planner. "I went into business," she says. "I was never inspired to go into television or theater." Five years of that led to a brief stint in New York City, where she helped her younger sister in a financial

Strategic Spending

To Hildi, successful design involves quality, not quantity.

When you're working with a limited decorating budget, Hildi recommends buying quality, not quantity. On the show, she usually spends the majority of her money on a single focal point element. "Design your room with intent," she says. "Think about what is going to make the biggest impact." For example, in a Chicago bedroom, Hildi spent big bucks for exotic Brazilian wood to make a new platform bed. In another bedroom she earmarked money for red toile.

Don't be afraid to go for one big-ticket item; the rest of the room design will evolve from that specially chosen object or element. The same is true when buying a wardrobe: Why waste a limited budget on a bunch of cheap items? Hildi recommends, "Buy something that is going to make the difference."

services firm catering to Latin American countries. Then she moved to Raleigh to work as a political campaign manager.

Eventually, numbers started to bore Hildi, and she found herself spending more and more time decorating houses for friends in Raleigh. It struck her that she could be getting paid for this skill, and in the late 1980s she started taking on clients. In 1989 Hildi and a friend founded Working Girls, an interior design business and workroom. Most interior designers don't have their own workrooms, but the control freak in Hildi didn't want to have to rely on someone else.

As satisfying as that business was, Hildi chose to move to Atlanta in 1996

to work with two colleagues designing and developing townhouses as Third Millennium Development, Inc. While creating cutting-edge interiors for clients, Hildi also sold the properties. She is still involved in the business, though to a lesser extent since becoming involved in *Trading Spaces* and moving to Paris.

Hildi's lack of formal design training

Hildi, here creating a pillow, has been project-oriented since childhood.

has never been an issue for her. "I ended up where my gift has been all my life," says Hildi. "I do not need a degree to do what I do. To me, interior design is one of those things—either you have it or you do not."

When a dear friend and furniture representative, Michelle Larrabee, recommended Hildi to the producers of *Trading Spaces*, they approached her about joining the show. The prospect of a cable TV decorating show wasn't immediately attractive to Hildi. She recalls what she told the producers: "If it is about design and two days, et cetera, I will tell you

Opposite: Hildi's take on traditional. **Below:** During the creation of and putting the finishing touches on a European-inspired kitchen. The walls were covered with 5,000 wine labels.

79

Hildi's Homage to Hildi

Hildi loves leaving her mark in the rooms she's created.

The rooms on *Trading Spaces* may belong to the homeowners, but they've been possessed by Hildi—and she doesn't mind if it shows.

✴ In the gray bedroom with the aluminum foil ceiling, Hildi adds a live yellow canary and names it "Hildi."

✴ In the quadrant living room, Hildi creates art by enlarging photographs that depict parts of her own body.

✴ In a Philadelphia living room, Hildi covers one wall with a colored-dot, Lichtenstein-inspired self-portrait of her head.

✴ In a European-flavor room, Hildi enlarges a photograph of the Eiffel Tower with her standing next to it. In fact, more than half of the rooms she designs for the show feature her own photography—images from around the world. "I leave a trail," she says. "I leave good things behind, I hope."

> ❝ I know what is behind a wall. I know how to use tools. Now, whether I want to do it, I do not know. ❞ —**Hildi** before joining the cast of *Trading Spaces*

why I think I can do it. I know what is behind a wall. I know how to use the tools. I know how to build a doghouse, change the oil in my car. Now, whether I want to do it, I do not know." After trying one episode, the novelty of the show and the challenge of the assignment became apparent. She saw *Trading Spaces* as a way of offering up thanks for her own creativity by sharing it with others. "The first show I did, that is all I could think about," she remembers.

Sometimes you have to wonder if Hildi is sharing too much of her creativity. Take the episode in which she covered the walls of a bathroom with fake flowers: During the shoot, boxes containing more than 6,000 silk flowers are stacked on the back patio. Everyone in the house knows what the plan is, but it's not until

the flowers are unpacked that the full, horrifying realization sinks in. As the flowers go up—stapling them takes hours—the caterers, camera operators, and homeowners are speechless. They pop in to check on Hildi's progress, then walk away shaking their heads. Hildi is oblivious. She thinks this is a fabulous idea. Gaffer's tape protects her palm, which is blistered from maniacal stapling.

Hildi knows the design is wild. She's not suggesting that viewers cover the wallpaper in their master bathrooms with thousands of silk flowers. Maybe they'll use silk flowers in a little girl's room. Or they might use baseball cards, decorative paper, or place mats in some other room. "Do not do it the way I did it," she says. "Take my idea and develop it your way." More than anything, Hildi wants to inspire viewers to take a risk. She is fighting against the mind-set that you should decorate in a certain style because that's the way everyone you know decorates. "*Trading Spaces* helps people snap out of that," says Hildi. "That is why I do it, to hopefully influence people and bring them out of their shell."

Hildi   Gen

Opposite: Silk flowers—more than 6,000 of them in all colors of the rainbow—adorn the walls of this bathroom. Stapling each individual flower to the walls took hours—and resulted in frustration and blisters.

81

> **"** We were awkward with the cameras at first, but then Gen was so easy to be with. She listens in a way that's so completely undivided, you feel chemistry. Soon it was like we were all just friends hanging out, having regular conversations, and the cameras just happened to be rolling. **"** —**David Smith**, Delta Upsilon fraternity (Berkeley: Prospect Street)

When Genevieve Gorder walks into a room, heads turn. It's not because she's instantly recognized as a *Trading Spaces* designer—that moment usually coincides with her giveaway giggle—and it's not solely because she's a tall, striking, green-eyed blond with a seductive strut. Her unmistakable allure lies instead in the way this good-gal designer brims with her own contented spirit.

Gen has the smirk of a girl who approaches every day as her birthday. She's prone to flirting and roaming barefoot and she hates symmetry. Despite some grunts about an early moss-covered wall, she's received rave reviews for rooms ranging from a Moroccan teen fantasy to bright, happy kitchens, a groovy "retrofly" lounge, and comfy, woodsy dens. She's found design inspiration in old cigar box labels, sliced vegetables, a homeowner's favorite sea-glass necklace, and a few brief tango lessons from an Argentinean cowboy named Orlando. Many have described Gen's style as eclectic and whimsical. The resident free spirit of *Trading Spaces* is anything but random in her mission to make America rethink white walls and beige carpet. "Decorating comes down to how

genevieve gorder

While some fans have referred to Genevieve Gorder as "The Barefoot Designer," flashing her feet on TV serves a practical purpose: Gen adores her collection of shoes and doesn't want them dappled with paint, adhesives, or numerous other materials she works with every day.

83

In Defense of Moss

Gen stands behind one of her most daring designs.

Gen makes no apologies for the only room in the history of *Trading Spaces* to be rejected before it was even seen. "Something smells," said the pair of San Diego homeowners before opening their eyes to see their bedroom wall covered in floor-to-ceiling moss. "That room was hot!" insists Gen, who's built five more moss walls on commission since that show aired. All were in Manhattan, where urbanites can appreciate portable greenery that grows without light or regular watering. "I'm sorry the San Diego homeowners didn't get it, and that they had allergies," Gen continues, "but at least I got someone out there thinking about the design merit of a material you won't see on a store shelf." To that end maybe her organic wonderland was a success: As they stapled on the unconventional wallcovering, Gen's team members were definitely thinking *"Why?"* They kept at it and got at least some viewers thinking *"Why not?"*

`01:32:09.25` `01:44:22.06` `01:46:08.00`

OK, so... enough about the moss!

you find your joy," she explains, "and I'm there to help make yours visible."

That joy can be tough to define when Gen's only contact with her homeowner client is a 20-minute video. Her solution? She mentally puts herself in her homeowners' place. Take the couple who enjoyed sitting by the fireplace in their cramped basement dreaming of a cozy cabin makeover: Gen conjured memories of autumns spent at her grandpa's Minnesota cabin and responded with

Lewis

Gen

Adrian

The always cheer-ful Gen with her two brothers

a design that included not only the look and feel of heavy timber but also the smells, tastes, and overall warmth of the season. She painted the walls to recall the cinnamon she remembers wafting from hot cider; she sewed pillows from 99-cent thrift store sweaters and a corduroy shirt (snap buttons, pockets, and all).

Coincidentally, it was also a shirt that inspired Genevieve's first decorating effort at the ripe age of 7. Taking a cue from her do-it-yourselfer parents who restored their share of south Minneapolis Victorian homes, Gen boldly drew up plans for her own custom headboard patterned after her favorite (and oh-so-'80s) T-shirt, which boasted a bright rainbow arching up one sleeve and down the other. She had some help building that masterpiece, but by high school Gen's family experiences on house projects had instilled within her the know-how to strip wood, varnish, lay tile, and take down wallpaper by herself.

> **She really does dance spontaneously—but only to one or two songs on every CD that she says are upbeat enough for the spirit of the room, and after that she's up again to change the music every two songs.** —Jennifer Quinn (Missouri: Sunburst Drive)

Walls and floors soon took a backseat to hip-hop, soccer, and some ambitious language and cultural pursuits. Growing out of her embarrassing preteen permed bob and fascination for all things Cyndi Lauper (any surprise this girl just wanted to have fun?), Gen committed herself to studying Spanish and the violin. Both endeavors stemmed not from school requirements but from seeds planted by her parents, who wanted their children to see and embrace cultures the world over.

"We weren't conventional," says Gen's mom, "but we weren't hippies either. Arts and travel were about giving our kids the education they need to get out there in life and keep moving." Gen's mom is co-owner and instructor of a yoga studio as well as a women's health nurse practitioner and former modern dancer. Her dad and brother Lewis are talented amateur photographers, her stepdad a classical bassist, and

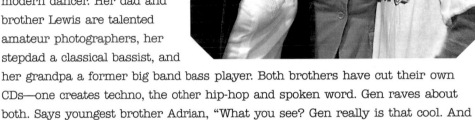

her grandpa a former big band bass player. Both brothers have cut their own CDs—one creates techno, the other hip-hop and spoken word. Gen raves about both. Says youngest brother Adrian, "What you see? Gen really is that cool. And more. She's all about family. I know I can count on her."

> "Who would I hang out with? All of them. Brains, geeks, jocks, the artsy crowd, and yeah, Molly Ringwald. But I'd always date the skateboarder."

The always reliable Gen learned at a young age to follow her own dreams with a sensible mix of caprice and drive. She traveled as far as France (twice) to play violin with her youth orchestra and, during a summer break in high school, studied as an exchange student in Barcelona, Spain. While she debated world politics and contemplated life in the foreign service, a poster of Prince in *Purple Rain* hung above her bed. (She's still a huge fan.) Asked whom she would have hung out with if she had been a character in the film *The Breakfast Club*, Gen answers, "All of them. Brains, geeks, jocks, the artsy crowd, and yeah, Molly Ringwald. But I'd always date the skateboarder. Probably for his sense of adventure," she muses.

College brought Gen to Portland, Oregon, where besides breathing in that first fateful scent of Oregon moss, she majored in international affairs at Lewis and Clark College. Passionate about world cultures but weary of memorizing political science acronyms, she enrolled in art classes, eventually finding her calling in a graphic design class. "It all just clicked. Everything changed," she recalls. Her newfound talent landed her an internship at MTV in New York City, which later

High school days

Pretty in pigtails

Nice socks, Gen

Gen's snapshots showcase the evolution of a free-spirited trendsetter. **Clockwise from left,** Gen drying off after a swim, breaking hearts in high school, strolling the beach (in high style!), and acting coy in grade school.

Minnesota

Welcomes You

Home Sweet Home

Top row: Question-and-answer sessions and autograph signings at the home and garden trade show. **Second row:** Gen and her family kicking back in the hotel between Gen's appearances.

became a full-time job; soon she dropped out of Lewis and Clark to start over at the School of Visual Arts in Manhattan. Working and studying full-time, she followed that fast track all the way back to Amsterdam in the Netherlands.

Landing back in New York, Gen found work with an award-winning studio called Duffy Design. Her credits there include the bottle and label on Tanqueray 10 bottles, but her interests strayed toward three-dimensional graphic design. As she explains it, that means she might design a logo for a company, then its exhibition booths, and maybe its

corporate T-shirts or benefit dinner menus. "It all comes down to color, form, balance, and knowing your materials. You use them all to flesh out a character," she says.

Gen's description of three-dimensional graphic design isn't too far from her current idea of a successful room makeover—materials,

Gen and a homeowner try to decipher manufacturer's instructions.

color, form, and balance all come into play in home decorating. Back when *Trading Spaces* called, Gen had yet to see the connection between graphics and interior design. "I grew up with *Designing Women* and just didn't think decorating was cool. I pictured all interior designers wearing big perfumed scarves and bursting through swing doors balancing bolts of purple chintz," she explains. Never saying no to the possibilities of serendipity, she got on a plane. Gen recalls, "They sent me a copy of *Changing Rooms* [the British TV series that inspired *Trading Spaces*], and I thought, I could do that." She auditioned along

genevieve gorder

Born: July 26, 1974
Raised: Minneapolis
Adopted Hometown: New York City
Favorite Saying: "That's so sick!" (a compliment)
Addictions: Tortilla Española and MAC lip glass
Most Embarrassing Moment: During an interview on the *Today* show, she quipped "Matt, I can do anything for $1,000."
Photographed at Le Souk, New York City on November 7, 2002

with what she says felt like 3,000, but in the middle of a crowd, she knew deep inside that the moment was hers.

Now on the road for *Trading Spaces* every month, Gen has her own reality-based platform to break down that old TV stereotype of interior decorators. Her greatest pet peeve? Rooms that are all image and no comfort. "That's what makes design look petty," she argues. Meaningful design to her mind is "experiential." It means embracing memories and passions and dissecting them for hints of color, form, smells, and texture: Remembering an island honeymoon, for instance, and asking yourself, "What color of blue was that water?"

A strong desire to savor a moment is what drove Gen to blindfold one of her little brothers on his sixteenth birthday and drive him to Niagara Falls,

Design Solutions the Gen Way

What do a gorgeous garnet ring, a steaming bowl of Thai chicken soup, and a box of Cuban cigars all have in common? They've all inspired Gen's room designs. Some other unlikely inspiration sources:

Problem	Inspiration	Solution
A girly bedroom in pastel hues and saccharine-sweet florals puts a cramp in the recent engagement of a fun-loving, 20-something Missouri couple.	**The romance of gauchos** (cowboys of the Argentine pampas)	A gender-friendly love nest where hard edges and leather straps mingle with luscious red roses, deep earthy walls, and a favorite painting of a sexy pink lady in a big, Baroque gold frame.
A Colorado couple with a passion for food and entertaining long for a kitchen with more zest than the bland white and gray palette they've cooked up.	**An artichoke** (boiled and peeled)	Bright plum wine walls based on the colorful heart of an artichoke speak "vigor, food, life" against the soft, faded, leaf green of vanilla-sage cabinets and black accents of appliances, pots, and pans.
With a big TV and a floating keg refrigerator, a Philadelphia husband's basement sanctuary looks more like a collection of his wife's throwaways than his own functional, masculine style.	**A Scrabble game board**	A man's play station in handsome taupes and browns featuring painted grids, a wall-length wet bar, framed gameboards, and "triple word point" pillows made by sewing black stars onto pink pillows.
A cavernous bedroom in a New Orleans neighborhood of recent construction needs a "big easy" dose of one-of-a-kind character.	**None. Nada. Zip.**	So-so shabby chic. Laments Gen, "Without an inspiration point, I felt like I was mocking a style that already existed. Not my favorite room."

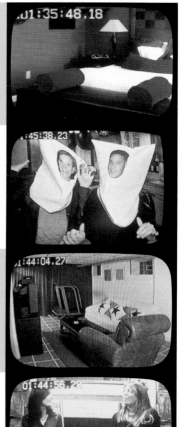

I'll have the soup du jour with a touch of modern sophistication, please. Consistent with most of her redecorating projects, Gen's design for this Washington, D.C., living room had an unusual inspiration—a steaming bowl of Thai noodle soup. The warm yellow walls and window treatments hint at a savory broth; the wicker ottomans, framed art, and sisal floor coverings mimic the tight texture of the noodles. Throw in a dash of red and russet pillows for spice, and the result is a room that hits the spot.

> **I think it's important whenever you do something that's remotely hip...that you are able to update. Otherwise you're stuck in something that becomes very passé.**

revealing the spectacular scene before him at the exact minute of his birth. "Gifts are gifts, but a sight like that will stay with you forever," she beams. Her passion also fuels an almost evangelical drive to make audiences take a utility knife to their family photos—an integral part of almost all Gen's rooms. The majority of episodes feature Gen cropping or manipulating a homeowner's snapshots, inspired by the conviction that a whole scene is not half as resonant as an enlarged look at the corner of someone's smile.

Children's art also fuels her creativity because it's authentic. Thinking like an adult is limiting, according to Gen, whose goal is to approach objects and materials with the same

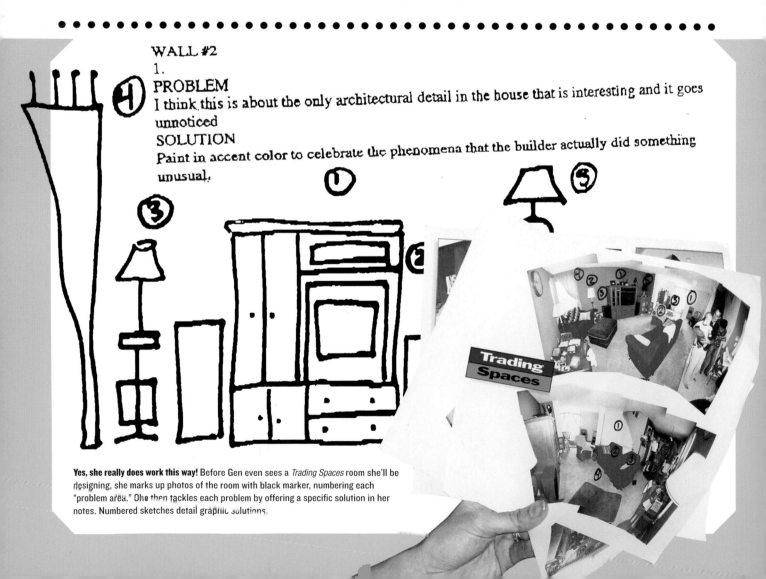

WALL #2

1.

④ PROBLEM
I think this is about the only architectural detail in the house that is interesting and it goes unnoticed
SOLUTION
Paint in accent color to celebrate the phenomena that the builder actually did something unusual.

Yes, she really does work this way! Before Gen even sees a *Trading Spaces* room she'll be designing, she marks up photos of the room with black marker, numbering each "problem area." She then tackles each problem by offering a specific solution in her notes. Numbered sketches detail graphic solutions.

The homeowners of this living room were not afraid of bold color—they just needed to unify the room's look. Gen's selection of bold Scandinavian hues now has visual "pop" against snow white woodwork and trim.

before

sense of play that allows a 6-year-old to invent 100 games from the same cardboard box. This approach is what made Gen see a man's tie as a curtain tieback (a pun, no less); it's also how she got the idea to turn a tall shelving unit on its side and add wheels to create a mod coffee table. "I hate shopping," she laments while speeding up her cart and jumping on to catch a brief ride. "It's just not creative. You're always working from what's in front of you rather than from your imagination."

Staying open to inspiration means being flexible. Gen's own apartment walls have seen five colors during the last four years. She rearranges her furniture often. At the moment, her favorite color is a desert red, warm and almost orange. She saw it first in Morocco and recognized it again while driving through New Mexico. A self-proclaimed gypsy, Gen spends her downtime either

Back to the hotel after a long day taping another episode

traveling or planning her next big trip. Prague is next, or maybe Cuba. Though not an avid souvenir collector, she has a small bull collection that includes a special find taken from a Barcelona wall. Instead of tearing off the latest bullfight

94

Gen's Top 5 Mood Enhancers

Lighting	Often overlooked, it's the first part of a room to affect your brain's level of happiness-inducing serotonin. Kill the overhead or add a dimmer switch. Think accent lamps and sconces.
Metals	From romantic silver to sleek chrome, every room needs a little polish. No metal in sight? Buff some cream-based metallic polish on anything that tickles your fancy.
Photography	No, not that stiff, cucumber pose you strike in front of monuments to document trips to distant cities; instead, snap and frame artful remembrances of defining lines, curves, and experiences.
Children's Art	Crop it, frame it—and face it, it's usually more imaginative than anything an adult mind could conceive.
Travel	Stay in one place your whole life and what have you got? One palette. Keep on the move and on the lookout for inspiration and color.

advertisement, she patiently chipped away at its edges to remove layer upon layer of posters at one time. They now hang stuck together on her apartment wall as an archaeological homage to the traditional Spanish pastime.

As for what Genevieve may attempt tomorrow, all you can expect is to be surprised. The only designer to don roller skates in order to paint a ceiling, Gen enjoys how *Trading Spaces* has given her the freedom to grow and expand her own design studio (self-named gg Studios). Her own line of hip greeting cards is a success, and she has big hopes for a new line of blue jeans. Others might consider Gen a dabbler in different industries, but she sees continuity in every venture. Asked by a college freshman what design classes she

Off-camera, candy-red heels put a bounce in her step.

should take for a career like Gen's, Gen answers, "Study everything—not just design but history, languages, math—and travel. Be a strong person; then you can be a strong designer."

On the set, Gen is fun-loving but focused. Meeting fans, shopping for dynamite accessories, filming how-to segments, and swapping designer horror stories with Edward are all part of the daily grind.

vern yip

If *Trading Spaces* were a Western, its smallest designer would wear the biggest white hat. Always gallant and seldom laid-back, the heroic Vern Yip typically arrives in town a full day early, eager to please another pair of homeowners.

Today Vern comes armed with pre-pinned fabrics, directions tracing the most efficient shopping itinerary, and at least a dozen copies of his 1,700-word, single-spaced episode manuscript outlining every organizational detail of a room's imminent transformation. As Vern distributes his dense handouts to a new homeowner team, key crew members, and one soon-to-be-busy carpenter, he jokes, "Please turn to page 67," revealing how well-prepared he is to laugh at himself and his unrelenting need to overachieve.

"Remember that annoying kid in school who was always asking the teacher for extra credit? That was me," Vern confesses. True enough, but that same kid also managed to earn four yearbook popularity titles, including "Most Sophisticated" and "Most Artistic," and he was also elected senior class vice president.

Vern is unmistakably driven, sometimes even competitive. Yet his demeanor remains more calming than clawing. He has a warm, inviting manner, a soft baritone voice, and a gift for diplomacy that swells from a well of good intentions. While

And not a curve in sight: All-around good guy Vern Yip straddles the line between art and science at one of his favorite buildings, The Salk Institute for Biological Studies in La Jolla, California.

Meeting Vern's Standards

If Vern's sleek, minimalist design style makes you thrill, take a crash course in Yip-ology. You may not have Vern's degree in architecture, but at least you can have his look.

Good	Bad
Mondrian	Romanesque
Formfitting, muscle-baring polo shirts	Loose, droopy drawers
Le Corbusier club chair	Puffed-arm couches in busy floral chintz
Lean grilled chicken for every meal	Sloppy joes and all-you-can-eat buffets
Repetition	Fluctuation
Clean, pressed sheets and dinner	Rumpled duvets
A yellow Lab puppy (man's best friend)	Snakes (too hissy, not to mention wavy)
Controlled, monochromatic palettes	A Mardi Gras parade
One perfect piece	10,000 tchotchkes

Now was that ³⁄₃₂" or was it ⁵⁄₃₂"?

shopping at a discount home store, he checks name tags and addresses employees by name when he has a question. After not finding what he was looking for, he diligently returns his empty cart to the front entrance, explaining "But if I didn't, someone would have to…"

Vern extends his good manners to his interiors. He cares deeply about his profession and sees it as a service, so he will go to great lengths to incorporate elements of other people's tastes into his own lean, linear designs. A minimalist at heart, he looks physically uncomfortable strolling the artificial flower aisles for materials to use in a crafts project. He's meticulous and has strong opinions on what's fussy. Asked why he wears muscle shirts, Vern answers, "I hate excess fabric. It looks messy, not clean." Yet this zealot for clean lines and smooth, solid planes always manages a smile, even when working with a homeowner's favorite busy toile fabric, walls inscribed with verses of sentimental poetry, and even distressed furniture.

Whether it's a *Trading Spaces* room or the 120-page report on Switzerland he submitted to a surprised sixth-grade teacher, Vern wants to do a job that will knock a homeowner's socks off. But living in overdrive can present its own challenges. Despite dissenting comments from fans, Vern remains convinced that a looming, 5-foot-diameter clock face was the right bedroom decoration for a young Long Island woman seeking

Vern differs from many decorators, whose designs spring from the color or style of a particular object or textile. His inspiration comes from the structure of the room itself and from the architecture of its contents. "I like to pull it all together by line rather than pattern," he explains.

solace away from the hustle and bustle of the office. After all, with candles mounted in place of each number, the clock face made light (literally) of fleeting time.

Vern's clock is perhaps testimony to how he's made peace with his own sleepless drive. *Trading Spaces* is his moonlighting gig, a pursuit of passion. He enjoys the challenge of budget and time constraints, which teach him to think in new ways. When he's not scrambling to redo a room for $1,000, Vern can spend that amount on a single lampshade for one of his private clients. As head

of his own company, a posh Atlanta-based architecture and interior design firm, he's designed spaces for crowd-pleasing restaurants as well as reclusive rock stars. And despite the time demands of television and his growing fan base, he sees no reason to slow the accelerating pace of his business.

Vern credits his strong, enterprising spirit to an

inspiring family of self-made individuals. His father was a successful soccer player (he played on the Chinese national team) and biochemist turned businessman. Vern's mother graduated from China's premier university—the only woman in her class. Settled in

99

Hong Kong, the Yips chose to emigrate with their children, 10-year-old Katherine and 2-month-old Vern, to start over again in the United States. Soon after arriving in the U.S., Vern's mom found herself running her own successful company, becoming an international consultant for developing industries. Several decades later, Katherine returned to Hong Kong, where she started and runs a dynamic business concentrating on designing and manufacturing home decor items, furniture, clothing, and specialty items for the doll industry. Says Vern, "If you think I work hard, you should meet my sister."

Vern was still quite young when Katherine left for college. With full run of the house and no sibling to rival, Vern thrived. He discovered his own hobbies and pursued them at his own exacting pace. His first passion was for dinosaurs, which he saw at the nearby Smithsonian National Museum of Natural History. Forget the cartoon versions: Toddler Vern lined his shelves with realistic miniature models. By

100

Above: Vern and a homeowner work together to make precise cuts for a paneled wall treatment. **Below:** City slicker Vern has a "hay"-day in rural Indiana.

Vern's Design Building Blocks

Vern prefers to build up a room from its framework of defining lines and forms, focusing on seven aspects:

Line

Think edgy—from the edges of your furniture and your windows to the edges where walls meet the ceiling or floor. In Vern's book, the sharper those lines, the cleaner the look.

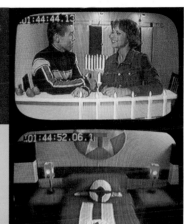

Perspective

Every room has lines and every line a direction; you're their matchmaker. Horizontals are desperately seeking verticals for balance or diagonals for some action. Follow the dominant direction of a room to the place where all lines converge, and that's where not to put your cat's litter box. Vern suggests reserving the spot for a spiffy art project instead.

Forms

Most shapes, or forms, need a little breathing space. A basket of green apples adds color, but lined up à la Vern in single file on a shelf, those apples will draw the eye as if they were sculpture.

Materials

Vern wants to see materials used "honestly"—with natural textures and colors speaking for themselves. He's patterned walls with uniform, square cuts of wood by simply alternating the direction of the wood grain; he's sparked some bedroom magic with cut-glass ornaments; and he's played it cool with smooth glass, sleek metals, and sultry silk.

Color

Vern isn't shy about using bold colors, but for peace of mind, he prefers using one at a time. Different shades of that one hue are OK. Try reversing your adjectives to expand your palette: Purply red works with reddish purple and grayish blues with bluish grays. White, black, grays, and noncolors such as reflective glass and shiny metals are fine too.

Art

Blessed with a monochrome palette, anything goes. Make the most intimate, personal choices with art because you're no longer confined by the need to match a painting to the color of your couch. But freedom doesn't mean scattering your art everywhere: Placement is key. Says Vern, "If you love a piece of art, I want to be able to walk in a room and understand the importance of its presence for you."

People

The most essential, most dynamic element of any room. Rooms are a canvas for how you live your life, according to Vern, so if conversation is what you want from a space, don't seat your friends on a busy floral couch. "Too distracting," he warns. Again, placement counts. Pull your family room sofa away from the wall to show the central importance of gathering or hide that daybed away in a restful nook for easy cocooning.

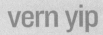

vern yip

Born: June 27, 1968
Raised: Washington, D.C., suburbs
Adopted Hometown: Atlanta
Addictions: Diet Coke and the adjective "sweet"
Personal Heroes: Mutant X-Men, IM Pei, and Mom
Dislikes: High fives and anything with mayonnaise
**Photographed at The Salk Institute for Biological Studies,
La Jolla, California on November 15, 2002**

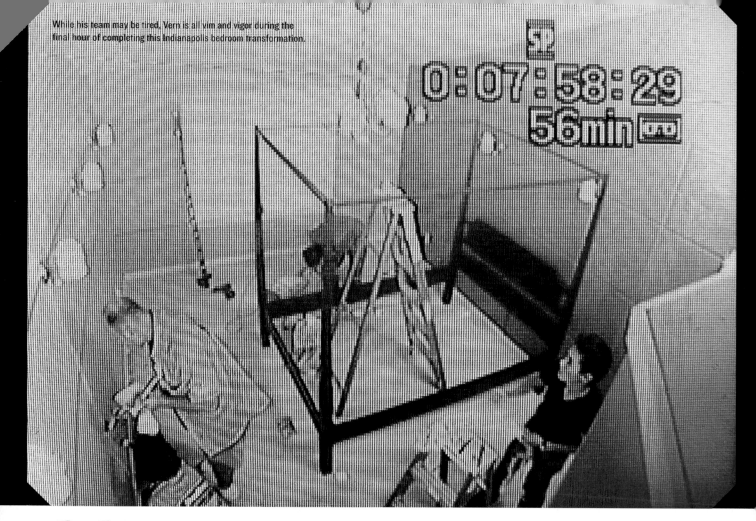

While his team may be tired, Vern is all vim and vigor during the final hour of completing this Indianapolis bedroom transformation.

0:07:58:29 56min

> ## "I had the world's largest Lego set. Houses, skyscrapers, cities— I had to erect structures. Never toys or cars."

kindergarten he had committed to memory the genus and species of each one. Then came Legos. Recalls Vern, "I had the world's largest Lego set because I couldn't tear anything I built down. Houses, skyscrapers, cities—I had to erect structures. Never toys or cars."

Next came a chemistry set, then fish. By second grade he was learning how to balance salt levels in their tank. "I made mistakes," admits Vern. "I killed a lot of fish." By fourth grade, Vern was busy amassing a comic book collection—5,000 issues he kept alphabetized in archival plastic sleeves, along with their current price guide. His favorite series was the X-Men. "The lines were crisp, the color

palette clean, and everything precisely inked," raves Vern. "Even then I knew what I liked."

If one sight alone solidified Vern's artistic vision, it would have to be his first trip to the National Gallery of Art. Young Vern couldn't get enough of milling around the galleries of the East Building, designed by architect

True blue: Vern's team carefully applies a coat of paint.

IM Pei. Standing in the atrium of the gallery, Vern was transfixed by its dynamic lines as well as the sense of harmony created among the building, the art, the flow of people, and the surrounding landscape. He loved how surfaces so plain could

104

after

before

Vern took this bedroom fireplace from blah to breathtaking without busting his budget. Glass trinkets hang from a simple metal frame, while martini glasses moonlight as tea light holders.

be so decorative: marble floor tiles, panes of glass, steel scaffolding, concrete blocks, and the expanse of lawn and sky outside. "That building is so pure and honest, it moves you emotionally from inside or out," says Vern, who knew then he wanted to be an architect.

In seventh grade, Vern drew up plans for an addition to his family's house (plans that his parents actually used), and designed a glass and chrome furniture set that his mom ordered to be custom-built for his room a year later. In high school,

between soccer, wrestling, polo, high school peer counseling, and his Elizabethan singing group, design was simply another of Vern's hobbies. When it was time to choose a career, he traveled the path established by his first chemistry set, following it all the way to premed studies at the University of Virginia. Graduating with a double major in economics and chemistry, Vern applied to medical schools and was accepted. But two weeks before starting, he suddenly backed out.

A rare moment: Vern actually sits down during a *Trading Spaces* shoot.

> **" Try walking into a room with a million different colors. Maybe you're wearing a pink shirt and brown pants—that makes you colors number a million one and a million two. People are more important than that. "**

Think one color for an entire room is boring? Think again. Vern used a rich palette of reds—in various textures, sheens, and intensities—in this Washington, D.C., bedroom to inject life and unify the space.

He interned at an architectural firm instead, pouring cup after cup of coffee and hoping to learn enough about drafting to build a portfolio. Four years later, he graduated from Georgia Tech with Masters degree in Architecture and an M.B.A. One of his first jobs was designing the offices for Disney Cruise Line, but before that he had started with the basics— for example, designing the toilet details that no established architect wanted to do. One day while Vern was working on this humble project, a principal of the firm looked over his shoulder at his drawings and

said, "You'd make a great interior designer." Vern had to agree.

In time he joined the offices of a prominent Atlanta design firm, then went out on his own. He studied technical aspects that weren't a part of his architectural training and passed the registration exam for board-certified interior designers. Working as both an architectural and interior designer, Vern loves knowing that he can detail your gutters one minute, then pick out your bedspread the next. But, mostly, he loves how the two fields give him multiple avenues for solving problems of form and function—and he is undeniably efficient in his solutions: The upholstered cushions that he hung in a row on a Chicago kitchen wall can function as wall art, extra seat cushions, or seat backs for a backless bench. Vern will never be like decorators whose room designs spring from the color, spirit,

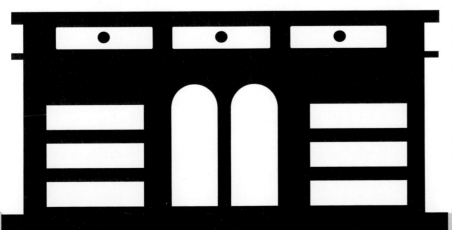

107

Big Kid Vern

Grown-up Vern toys around with design when decorating for kids.

Many people, designers included, use children's rooms as an excuse to go wild with color and cartoon character bedsheets. But the designer famous for obsessing over angles and elevations takes a different, cleaner approach. Vern's rooms for children are impeccably ordered and geometrically precise, featuring limited color and installations so tedious they recall the seriousness of playing architect with Erector sets, or hostess to a table of stuffed friends at a tea party. Says Vern, "I view a kid's room as a sanctuary, a place to escape, sleep, play, and dream. To make space for all that activity in a room, you can't crowd every corner. What you really need to do is take a step back." From prekindergarten on up, little Vern practiced transforming empty playspaces into orderly galleries of dinosaurs, Lego cities, and finally comic books. By his preteen years, the aspiring sophisticate had painted his walls a solid slate gray and designed his own suite of contemporary glass and chrome furniture. Remembers Vern, "My sister walked in one weekend and screamed, 'Your room looks like a bank vault!'"

or style of a particular object or textile. His inspiration comes from the structure of the room itself and from the architecture of its contents. "I like to pull it all together by line rather than pattern," he explains. "Pattern is just too distracting."

Since joining the show late in the first season (after an introduction by fellow Atlanta designer Hildi), Vern has maintained a steadfast policy: "If you're my homeowner, you're the same as my client." Ever a people person, Vern maintains that he's pen pals with all his past homeowners. This attitude of commitment helps explain why Vern is so adamant about making $1,000 look like $10,000, and why mood is the most important effect he strives for. One *feng shui* room gave him a rap for quiet, meditative spaces (a reputation Vern blames on the stereotyping of Asian

design). In reality Vern's designs are as dynamic as they are peaceful. "The two are not contradictory," he insists, which is no surprise coming from a dynamo whose boundless energy stirs below a calm, cool manner.

Occasionally, however, that energetic core shows itself in a frantic outburst. The designer with a reputation for being Mr. Nice, Vern's installations can be exacting and

Vern loads his shopping cart for another room redo.

his sets tenser than average. If this otherwise amiable guy isn't a barrel of laughs every second, fans don't care. Vern never demands more than half of what he's willing to give himself, and if he gets worked up, it's only because he's working so hard to please everyone around him.

A lifelong comic book fan, Vern does his best Aquaman impersonation (and gets along swimmingly with a new dolphin buddy) during a visit to SeaWorld in San Diego.

109

> **"** I like repetition, symmetry. There's nothing wrong with the unexpected, but I like knowing what's going on and what to expect. Sometimes jumping off a building, designwise, is not practical or comfortable—it's going for shock value. **"**

Ever since his first episode working as a behind-the-scenes sewing coordinator, Edward Walker felt he would be perfect as an on-camera designer for *Trading Spaces*. "I wanted to be the one making decisions," says Edward. "I'm tailor-made for this." During the second season of the show, he toiled away in Sewing World (see page 7), stitching up curtain panels and dust ruffles for Hildi, Doug, and the rest, all the while keeping his own designer ambitions mostly to himself. He did tell a camera operator, and eventually he told Paige. He also told Frank, who was very supportive, but says Edward, "I didn't mention it to any of the other designers."

When the popularity of the show precipitated more episodes and the need for two new designers, Edward lobbied for an audition. Though he had an in, his chances were slim. After all, here's a guy with an art degree, a fashion degree, and an established career designing and sewing couture gowns; everyone knew him as the sewer, as one of the crew—not one

edward walker

After serving as a behind-the-scenes sewing coordinator for the first two seasons of *Trading Spaces*, Edward Walker landed a designer position. He doesn't view the new position as a step up or down: "Everybody's important in getting the job done. We're all in this world together." Above: With fellow designer Laurie.

I'm sorry, but I just don't do ugly.

Mom

Carl

Edward

Dad

of the talent. After he pulled off a successful camera test, producers were still concerned about his lack of an interior design degree. "I don't make any bones about having a degree," says Edward, who has had interior design clients over the years. "To me, design is design. If you understand color, balance, and scale, that's the whole thing." During an episode, Edward puts it more succinctly, speaking in his Southern drawl: "I don't do ugly."

Defying expectations is nothing new for Edward. He spent much of his childhood in Whiteville, North Carolina, where, as in many small towns, football is king. Dad was a Southern Baptist minister, and Mom was a college counselor (they met at seminary). Younger brother Carl grew up to work as a cardiovascular blood perfusionist. Then there was Edward. "I was a different commodity," he says while lying on a homeowner's den floor an hour after a Reveal upstairs. The camera crew steps over him as they move equipment out. He has been up for nearly 48 hours, and although his clothes are still pristine, his eyes are starting to show some fatigue. He's completely spent. He ponders his youth: When the other kids were out hootin' it up, he, a then-introverted minister's kid, sequestered himself in his room, sketching designs and making every do-it-yourself project he could get his hands on. "I was very old for a high school student," he says. "I didn't have

Dad

Edward

Always dapper, even at age 4 Edward never had a bad suit.

112

Hair Flair

From head to toe, Edward is always perfectly groomed.

Unlike Doug, who sports various hair poufs, flips, and flops, Edward wears the same hairstyle show after show: shaved sides with the rest pulled back into a neat ponytail. "Paige says it looks like I'm wearing some sort of cap," he says. "My hair is a big issue." The issue is manageability. When Edward wears his thick, coarse hair short, he has to use

hair products, blow-dry it, and get it cut every single week, which isn't an option when you're living on the road. It's easier to wear it long. When he started going gray, he shaved the sides because the hair there grew out in tufts. Says Edward, "It sticks out like Grandpa's on *The Munsters*."

Southern Charm: Edward is unfailingly well-mannered. Courtesy and etiquette are his guiding principles in dealing with others. He displays the same level of courtesy toward everyone, whether it's the local caterer, the homeowners, or the producer of the show.

time for goofing around."

His mother's extensive wardrobe and his grandmothers' sewing skills tipped Edward's creativity toward fashion. More than anything, he wanted to study fashion design in New York. His parents always encouraged their children to be individuals, but they also stressed the importance of education. So Edward first went off to North Carolina's Wingate University for an art degree. His senior project? Five evening gowns, five watercolor paintings of the gowns, and five watercolor and quilted-fabric screens. After working a year in retail and a year as a teacher, Edward headed for the Fashion Institute of Technology (FIT) in Manhattan. "Here I was this little country hick," he says. "New York opened my eyes. It was life-changing." Instead of being the arty oddball in his small, sports-crazed town, Edward was finally surrounded by people who shared his interests. He flourished.

After graduating from FIT, he worked for two years as a junior designer, then landed a top job designing beaded gowns at another mother-of-the-bride fashion house.

Edward's gowns

With a draper and four seamstresses in his charge, he created 200 gowns a year. "And if you design 200, you draw 1,000," he says. He also produced catalogs, choosing the models and styling the sets.

His job allowed him to travel the world several times over: He went to China, where the gowns were made and beaded; to India, where beading was also done; to France and Germany for fabrics and inspiration; and that's only a sampling of his itinerary. He loved the job, but it got to be too much. New York's demanding fashion scene, combined with frequent globe-trotting stints, made Edward

long for a simpler life, a life with a car, a yard, and a nice Southern gal. So, after a youth spent trying to escape North Carolina, Edward returned to his roots, settling in Raleigh with a custom formal-wear business he runs from home. "I don't need to go to any more cocktail parties. How many times can you work a room selling a line and still get enjoyment out of it?" he says. "I was able to come back to a much more comfortable life."

Edward (never Ed, Eddy, or The Edmaster) exhibits none of the casual, rough-and-tumble vulgarities of contemporary pop culture. He seems to come from another age, and it's easy to imagine him walking down

Top: Planning and shopping with "Fast" Eddie, the carpentry assistant, and Frank, and going it alone. **Bottom:** Filming a craft project with Paige and a homeowner.

from the screen of a 1940s film. Here's why:

Edward is always impeccably groomed. During a quick dash to Carpentry World (see page 7 for more), he bends down to measure and mark out some wall plaques on plywood. His dark button-down shirt (long sleeves only) and tan slacks are perfectly pressed ("I even have to press my polo shirts before I wear them."). He wears good-quality shoes (Italian, of course), and they're polished—always polished. Accessories include a silver bracelet on one wrist, a watch on the other, and a silver ring on each hand. Wire-rimmed sunglasses are framed by dark hair, which is attractively gray at the temples and pulled back into a tidy ponytail.

Edward is unfailingly well-mannered. Courtesy and etiquette are his guiding principles in dealing with others. These are the marks of a Southern man from a religious family who believes that relationships with people are more important than money or getting ahead. He displays the same level of courtesy toward everyone, whether it's the local caterer, the homeowners, or the producer of the show. He gives his opinion only when asked. He listens attentively when

Edward sews *and* sculpts with scrap metal.

spoken to. He brings a baby gift for Laurie when she returns for her first episode after maternity leave.

Edward has penetrating eyes. Black brows and lashes around brown irises give him the dark and broody look of someone who is always thinking. Immediately after The Reveal on one house, he's thinking about his design for the next house. The constant

edward walker

Born: January 4, 1964
Raised: Whiteville, North Carolina
Adopted Hometown: Raleigh, North Carolina
Favorite Saying: "Build a bridge and get on over it."
Big Thrill: Roller coasters—the higher and faster, the better.
Ideal Woman: Southern, from a good family, with strong religious beliefs, attractive, communicative, intelligent, humorous, goal-oriented, independent, interested in the arts

Photographed in Austin, Texas on November 15, 2002

cadence in his head has made him an insomniac since childhood. He usually goes to sleep around 3:30 a.m. and wakes up at 9. If the air-conditioning repair person is coming at 7:30 a.m., Edward stays up all night.

There's something telling about Edward's decision to design formal wear instead of, say, swimsuits or jeans and sweatshirt combos. He's drawn to weddings—the ceremony, the ritual, the structure. "I love formality," he says. "Just about every part of my life is formal." He goes to a Southern Baptist church, but not the newfangled progressive kind where they sing a lot. He's old-school all the way. During Edward's childhood his family was always well-dressed; his father still wears a suit and tie every day. "I love to dress up myself, put on a tuxedo and go somewhere," he says. "That's fun to me."

In his interior design, Edward is unapologetically traditional. He doesn't do contemporary. He doesn't do eccentric. He feels most comfortable within the boundaries he grew up with, producing high-impact interiors that conform to commonsense rules. "I like repetition, symmetry," he says. "There's nothing wrong with the unexpected, but I like knowing what's going on and what to expect." When

Framing any item makes it seem more significant and artistic: your own primitive painting, enlarged photographs, pages from a calendar, plates from an art book. Go with a single, large piece or use a series of smaller items and display them in a row or grid.

he's designing rooms for *Trading Spaces*, Edward's goal is to create a room that functions well for the homeowners. In his opinion, avant-garde design doesn't have a place in interiors. You won't see him doing a Jackson Pollock paint job on the walls or throwing a mattress on the floor. "Sometimes jumping off a building, designwise, is not practical or comfortable—it's going for shock value," he says. Edward's rooms don't spark the controversy of Genevieve's moss walls, Hildi's flower bathroom, or Kia's hanging bed, and he doesn't want them to. He's quick to praise other designers for pushing the limit, but he wants his homeowners to like the room he designs and be able to live with it for the next five years. Says Edward, "If you're comfortable in your

> "To me, design is design. If you understand color, balance, and scale, that's the whole thing."

environment, that gives you the opportunity to be adventurous in other parts of your life."

Edward hopes that *Trading Spaces* viewers will glean some of his budget-wise project ideas. ("I am frugal down to the penny," he says.) And ideas abound in Edward's rooms. Take, for example, the bedroom with chocolate brown walls, a blue tray ceiling, and the bed positioned in the middle of the room. Edward's project list—16 in all—included a slipcovered headboard with a mantel top; lantern glass painted in the style of the fabric pattern; a duvet, a dust ruffle, and decorative pillows; a modified vanity table and a specially constructed entertainment unit with place mat door inserts; custom-made curtain rods fashioned from upholstered cardboard tubes and foam balls; new framed artwork; plywood shelves to hold Oriental accessories; an embossed wallpaper border on the tray ceiling; new paint on the dressers; refashioned reading lamps on the headboard; and hot-glued moss on a pot holding an uplit palm tree. All of which add up to two jam-packed days of hard work for himself, the homeowners, the carpenter, and the crew.

This tendency toward fullness shows up in Edward's own home, which features a mix of heirloom furniture, thrift store finds, sentimental items from his travels, images of gowns he has designed, and neoclassic busts and columns. "A decorator would

Yanni? No, it's Edward!

6 Tips for Beautiful Brides
Edward's advice on looking your best on your big day

Edward makes gowns of the same caliber as Vera Wang's or Carolina Herrera's. His dresses feature interlinings, linings, and interfoundations put together with couture finishing techniques. Distinguished by clean lines and wonderful fabrics, his designs are meant to draw attention to the woman. "I want people to say, 'She was a beautiful bride,' not, 'The dress was stunning,' " he says.

Tip 1 Match the dress style to the event. Don't wear a "big satin ball gown" if you're getting married on the beach and don't wear a "chiffon nothing dress" if you're getting married in a cathedral.

Tip 2 Select proper foundation garments. "You can build anything on a good foundation," Edward says. Wear the correct bra for the cut of the dress. Make sure figure-shaping garments have a smooth silhouette. Nothing should buckle or ripple when you bend or twist.

Tip 3 Don't waste money on designer shoes. If your gown is long, no one will notice your shoes anyway. Just make sure the shoes are either white or beige—and comfortable.

Tip 4 Choose appropriate jewelry. If your gown is simple, chunky or frilly jewelry is OK. If your gown is elaborate, keep jewelry to a minimum. "You don't do 'kitchen sink' on everything," says Edward.

Tip 5 Wear your hair in a classic style. Stick to a nice chignon or twist. "Get rid of curls and straggly doodad things," Edward says. "Curls don't last unless you have curly hair. And those little strings off to the sides drive me crazy."

Tip 6 Use a simple veil at the back of the head; Edward insists: "Those things with the poufs and the things all around and the pearls hanging down—oof, get rid of that." Go with a classic style that doesn't obscure your head or dress.

look at it and say, 'We need to pare down,'" he says. "Sometimes I have a tendency to overaccessorize, but there are things I don't want to part with." His entire house is painted in the Edward

With a fresh coat of paint, this dresser gets a new look.

give you clues about his personal preferences. "Each [room] is a reflection of myself," he says. Remember the den with the rug used as a wall hanging? Edward has a hanging rug in his house. And you know the ubiquitous decorative cording he uses as crown molding? Edward has hot-glued cording to the tops of the walls in every room of his house.

Edward's previous sewing position on the show gives an unusual perspective: Unlike the other designers on the show, he's worked with the entire cast and has experienced the quirks of each cast member's personality. When he started, he had the same questions everyone else does:

rainbow: brown, black, gray, beige, burgundy, gold, and metallic gold. However, over the past year, Edward has gotten a wild hair and is replacing the metallic gold items in his bedroom with metallic silver. The overall look is masculine; his home is not a bare, spare bachelor pad but a grown-up and tasteful space. Watching the show will

Conglomeration of Clothes

Edward's love of fashion extends, not surprisingly, into his own closets. Though he contends that he wears the same thing over and over, his jam-packed walk-in alcove and two closets tell a different story. "If I wore everything and didn't wash anything, I could probably get through a year," he says. His wardrobe includes, but is not limited to, the following items:

1 tuxedo	20 jeans	25 mock turtlenecks	20 pairs of cuff links
15 suits	30 dress slacks	38 sweaters	40 watches
10 blazers	25 turtlenecks	40 belts	40 pairs of shoes (25 of them black)

Do they really do it in two days? Is there a lot of ego and competition going on? "I was very surprised there weren't attitudes," he says. Edward thinks the other designers are exactly as they seem on-camera, but even nicer. "I've told Hildi this—I thought she might be a problem," says Edward. "She is very reserved on-camera and stoic. Once you get to know her, she's one of the funniest people off-camera I've ever met in my life. She's hysterical." Edward also says there's a camaraderie that comes from everyone working together and staying up late to meet a common challenge: "It's like a little family."

Landing the designer position has put him in an odd spot: Instead of taking orders, he's now giving them. He says, "I didn't know how some of the others would react. I'm sure in a way it's awkward for them as well." Still, halfway into the third season, Edward has continued as sewing coordinator during episodes when he isn't cast as a designer. "Wearing two hats—it's been tough," he says. "I'm just, like, confused—where am I supposed to be, and what hat am I supposed to be wearing at this time?"

Edward doesn't view the designer position as a step up or a step down. He falls back on his family's teachings to keep his newfound fame from going to his

A much needed break at the Indianapolis Motor Speedway

head. "Just because you may have some opportunities that other people do not, you don't set yourself above them," he says. "Everybody's important in getting the job done. We're all in this world together."

Good-bye, orange—and hello, sleek, cool, and classic. **Left:** One of Edward's neoclassic bedrooms. **Below:** Making it happen.

122

Edward's keen sense of style transformed a
traditional country bedroom, right, into a room
steeped in international refinement—with
neoclassic elements—above.

before

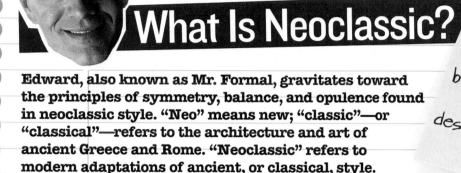

> Remember now... I don't do ugly.

What Is Neoclassic?

Strong geometric motifs, like circles, squares, and straight lines, are recurring themes in neoclassic style. For high style on a low budget, use these motifs as bold accents: Stencil the designs on walls, furnishings, and accessories.

Edward, also known as Mr. Formal, gravitates toward the principles of symmetry, balance, and opulence found in neoclassic style. "Neo" means new; "classic"—or "classical"—refers to the architecture and art of ancient Greece and Rome. "Neoclassic" refers to modern adaptations of ancient, or classical, style.

Neoclassic style became popular in the United States during the late 1800s, after the discovery of the ruins of Pompeii in Italy. Outside, a typical American neoclassic house has a two-story portico supported by columns with ornate capitals. There are numerous ways to achieve this style inside your home. Just follow these pointers:

✳ **Because strong geometric forms** are hallmarks of neoclassic style, furniture and accessories should be arranged symmetrically.

✳ **Pay attention to architectural details,** including columns, pediments, arches, wall niches, crown molding, paneled doors, and coffered ceilings.

✳ **Incorporate refined, rich surfaces,** such as polished marble, stone, and plaster, throughout your home.

✳ **Luxurious fabrics** can be used for everything from window treatments and bedding to slipcovers. Damask, brocade, silk, and velvet are the perfect choices.

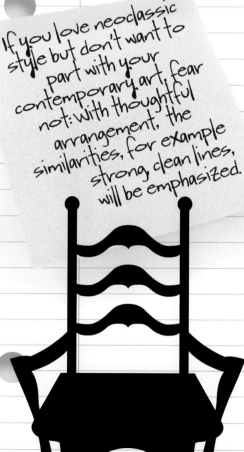

If you love neoclassic style but don't want to part with your contemporary art, fear not: With thoughtful arrangement, the similarities, for example strong clean lines, will be emphasized.

✳ **Structured window treatments,** including pleated draperies, stationary swags and valances, and jabots, work well in neoclassic-style rooms.

✳ **For added opulence,** select decorative rods and finials in colors that complement the treatments.

✳ **Accent soft furnishings**—for instance, pillows and curtain panels—with elegant details like tasseled cording for a regal feel.

✳ **Incorporate classic color schemes:** Try cream, soft yellow, and burgundy, dramatically accented by black, charcoal, and dark brown with liberal doses of gilt trim.

✳ **Accessories** pull the neoclassic look together: Select mosaics, murals, statues, busts, and pottery such as Wedgwood.

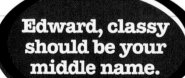

> Edward, classy should be your middle name.

kia steave dickerson

> **"It's hard being a woman in a man's world,"** says Kia, whose design business involves commercial construction. **"I tell them, 'Don't let this skirt and heels fool you, because I will climb this ladder, take this drill out of your hand, and do what I need to do.'"**

It's July 2002, and Kia Steave Dickerson is sitting expectantly in the center of a packed movie theater near her hometown. She's here for the Philadelphia premiere of *Signs*, the M. Night Shyamalan motion picture starring Mel Gibson, a project for which she worked props. People are smiling, chattering, and turning around to see others as Kia catches up with the rest of the prop department, many of whom she hasn't seen since shooting the film.

Positioning himself in front of the audience, Jose Rodriguez, an executive for Shyamalan's Blinding Edge Pictures, speaks with satisfaction of the finished film, then thanks everyone who worked on it. He reminds the audience that most of the stars are attending the New York premiere that's happening concurrently, but, he adds, there is one big star among them. People strain to see. Is it Mel? Joaquin Phoenix? Rory Culkin? Then Rodriguez announces that Philly's own Kia Dickerson is a new designer on *Trading Spaces*. A cheer goes out, and

Kia may have been more comfortable behind the camera than in front of it before *Trading Spaces*, but the camera loves her. Viewers can't wait to see what she'll wear or what she'll do.

Celebrity Spotlight

Hanging out with the rich and famous has unexpected benefits.

"Kia is the funk diva," says film writer and director **M. Night Shyamalan.** "She brings love, passion, and a singular style to everything she touches. She makes our movie sets more vibrant with her exotic electricity." On the set of Shyamalan's *The Sixth Sense,* Kia made tea every day for **Bruce Willis,** whose voice gets scratchy. He appreciated it so much, he provided all the exterior paint for her new house.

While filming *Signs,* **Mel Gibson** flew his private jet home to California every weekend. "He offered for anybody to go," recalls Kia, so she took him up on the offer. The flight included a tasty dinner (avocados, prawns, and Thai noodles) and some revealing comparisons of body piercings.

On the set of *Beloved,* **Oprah Winfrey** was rubbing Kia's head and joking to **Camille Cosby** how she, Oprah, was going to get her hair cut like Kia's. Kia doesn't ordinarily like to be touched, but she made an exception for her business idol, thinking to herself, "Kia, here's $453 million rubbing through your hair. Absorb the energy. Absorb the energy."

Writer/Director M. Night Shyamalan

Oprah, Patty LaBelle and Kia

Kia and Samuel Jackson

I don't take no stuff, from nobody.

audience members—Kia's friends—jump up in excitement and congratulations.

"Now that was an honor. That brought tears to my eyes," says Kia, completely surprised by the announcement and the reaction. "When you have people come forth and support you because you have enhanced and supported their life in some way—that's what success looks like to me."

Being singled out at a motion picture premiere is far from what Kia envisioned for herself as a youth. While attending West Catholic High School for Girls in Philadelphia, Kia questioned religious doctrine, prompting her occasional dismissal from class. Despite her rebellion, or maybe because of it, Kia performed well in school, excelling in business classes, where her entrepreneurial spirit blossomed. "I used to say in class that I was going to own my own business," says Kia. Her teenage mind, however, didn't know what that looked like—African-American business owners were few and far between. "The only person of color I could identify with was

Shopping: Kia makes a beeline to the crafts store for supplies. She's trying to explain to the sales gal what she wants. Kia: "You know those things that are wood and cylindrical and hollow; they have a hole in them so you can string things through them?" Sales gal: "You mean beads?"

George Jefferson, and he had a cleaners," she says. "So I always said I was going to have Kia's Cleaners."

Though TV's George Jefferson may have been a useful model of independence at that time, the adult Kia doesn't need a fictional character as her measure of success. For the past nine years, she has run K.I.A. Enterprises, a Philadelphia interior design firm primarily serving commercial clients that are refurbishing or building new facilities. At the same time, Kia works as an assistant prop master and set decorator for films, TV shows, and TV commercials. Her film credits include *12 Monkeys*, *Wide Awake*, *The Sixth Sense*, *Unbreakable*, *Men in Black*, and *Beloved*; her TV commercial set designs include spots for Betty Crocker, Chrysler, and Bisquick. "You've seen my work," she says. "You just didn't know it was me." On

the side, Kia also owns and runs several residential rental properties.

Always open to a new opportunity, Kia turned down a prop assistant job for Jennifer Lopez's *Jersey Girl* and accepted an offer from *Trading Spaces*

A trip to India—and a souvenir pair of hand-carved columns and brackets—inspired Kia's design concept for this room. Orange walls wrap the space in the color of Indian saris, which Kia used for runners and pillowcases. The focal point, however, is the hanging bed, suspended from the ceiling by chains. Opposite, above center: A wooden silhouette recalling the Taj Mahal frames the new entertainment center. Opposite, above right: An old baluster conceals the curtain rod.

First Sight: It's Kia's first look at her assigned master bedroom, and the room, as is, looks too good. "What am I doing here?" she asks, slumping to the floor, back to the wall. "I like what the owner has done here," she says, looking around, shaking her head. "It kind of throws you off."

executive producer Denise Cramsey. Kia joined the third season of *Trading Spaces* as one of two new designers (the other is Edward Walker). "It's exciting; it's fun; it feels very quirky," says Kia, who's finally getting used to being in front of the camera instead of behind it. "It's like, 'Huh? You want my autograph? For what?'"

During her first year on the show, Kia has demonstrated her flair for the theatrical. She wants to please the homeowners, of course, but her years behind the camera have taught her the importance of entertaining people. The color, furniture arrangement, and general theme of the room—that's for the homeowners. The pyramid fountain, the hanging bed, the camouflage table runner, the outfits that match the decorating theme of the room—that's for the television

The cast dons fatigues for an Air Force base room redo.

audience. Kia knows she's being gimmicky; she's trying her darnedest to be gimmicky. She's not concerned whether viewers like her designs, as long as

REC   PRIDE CAM

Around the Clock with Kia

From DIY at home to stadium-size projects, design is her life.

1:15 p.m. Sunday

I'm in my laundry room. I'm laying new flooring and I just got back from the home center with some beige, slate-looking vinyl tiles. It all started yesterday when I bought a new washer and dryer, that Kenmore Duet set with the front-loading washer. I went to the "scratch and dent" at the Sears outlet in Voorhees, New Jersey. They're usually $1,049 each, and I saved over $1,000 on the set. I never pay full price for anything. My old washer, from 1979, was here when I bought the house. I have a friend of mine here and a cousin here. We're all working.

10:30 a.m. Wednesday

I'm still in bed, wearing my suburban housewife fleece outfit—polar bears in purples, whites, pinks, and oranges. I need some extra rest. The laundry/mudroom turned into a whole thing. I laid new subfloor and vinyl tile, put a wallpaper border on the ceiling, and hung some mirrors because I'm putting a weight bench in there. I also pulled up some carpet my Rottweiler messed up. His name is Kew, for Kia, Elaine, and William. I'm watching TLC on TV and making phone calls. I'll work in bed for a while longer.

3:50 p.m. Monday

I'm driving from LAX to Lincoln Fabrics in Santa Monica to buy fabric for laminating some miniblinds for a *Trading Spaces* shoot out here. I'm on the 405 in LA, let me pull off.... I'm so excited because I just got a phone call saying I finally got work on the new Philadelphia Eagles football stadium. A partner and I have been trying to get that for 16 months. We're doing the wall surfaces, upholstery, and accessories for the 132 box suites. That's major for your resume. To do stadium work? That's huge. It's a milestone in my career to get to stadium status. You're talking an $800 million project, and I'm part of that.

they're entertained. She wants them to wonder "What in the world is Kia going to do this week?"

Case in point: Few viewers can imagine Vern creating a bedcover from artificial turf and silk flowers. Nope, that was a "Kia," and the design prompted both the homeowner who made it and the homeowner who received it to describe the bed as a grave. In the infamous episode, dressed in a getup of overalls and a straw hat, Kia made a last-minute change, adding even more silk flowers to the "resting place." Viewers squirmed, certain the homeowner was going to hate this whacked-out room with its brick lawn edging and gravel flooring. But to their astonishment, when the design was revealed, the homeowner actually liked—no, loved—the room. Now, that's good TV.

Kia, an only child, was raised by parents who unknowingly paved the way for her current career. Her father, William, the family's creative spirit, was a prop

Opposite and below: While shooting in Indianapolis, the cast couldn't pass up a chance to visit the Indianapolis Motor Speedway. Kia donned a helmet and squeezed into the backseat to see what sitting in those little Formula 1 cars really feels like.

kia steave dickerson

Born: Early 1960s
Raised: Philadelphia
Adopted Hometown: Philadelphia
Favorite Saying: "There's a method to my madness."
Sign: Capricorn. "I count my coins."
Proud Moment: In 2000, K.I.A. Enterprises received a citation from the city of Philadelphia for having a dramatic impact on the minority business community.
Risky Business: Tandem skydiving jumps from 14,000 feet
Photographed in Philadelphia, Pennsylvania on November 9, 2002

Kia with her mom and dad. **Below left,** Kia and her mom in matching pantsuits made by her father. The three were on their way to a Jackson Five concert.

" Somebody's going to have a Willy Wonka room," says Kia, "and I'm going to dress like an Oompa Loompa. "

master in the theater and a member of the local chapter of the International Alliance for Theater and Stage Employees (IATSE). "My dad was the first African American allowed in the local union after fighting to get in for 15 years," she says. As far back as Kia can remember, she was building, painting, and refurbishing with her dad, who would take her Dumpster™-diving for treasures. "My

134

mother used to say, 'Stop taking that baby picking trash!'" says Kia with a laugh. "But we had the coolest house on

the block." William, also an expert clothier, frequently decked out the family in—big surprise—theme outfits. If the Dickersons were doing a Southwestern activity, all three would wear fringed clothes, and William would don an eye patch. The opera? That was an occasion for William to sport a tuxedo, cape, and top hat; Kia and her

The African-American Walk of Fame in Philadelphia

mother wore evening gowns.

Kia's mom, Elaine, worked as a credit analyst, imparting to Kia her business sense. When Elaine brought work home, she would teach her little girl what she was doing. By eighth grade, Kia knew all about credit

OK

Touchstone Pictures and Blinding Edge Pictures
cordially invite you and a guest
to the special Cast & Crew screening of

si☉ns

Tuesday, July 30, 2002
8:00 pm

UA King of Prussia
300 Goddard Boulevard
King of Prussia, PA

RSVP to be admitted:

This invitation is non-transferable.

HOLLYWOOD
TAKE | SCENE
DATE
DIRECTOR

4 ANIMAL FACTORY
DANNY TREJO
WILLEM DAFOE (Marcus)

CONTAIN YOURSELF!

UTTERLY
BELOVED
12/17/97
1:45pm
OUR LAST
DAY AT
BLUE
STONE.

THE DICKERSON'S

Kia's Fridge

and the perils of being overextended, as well as how to write checks and balance a checkbook. Her parents pressured her to avoid design and get a "real job." Kia found she could mesh her interests with a program in textile design, marketing, and management at the Philadelphia College of Textiles and Science. College led to a series of jobs as a "glorified hustler," distributing wallpaper, window treatments, flooring, and fabrics for home furnishings. Then she started her own business. She takes a certain pleasure in occasionally reminding her mother of her advice, noting,

"Aren't you glad I didn't get a real job?"

Although Kia definitely works the system to create opportunities for herself, she's not all "me, me, me." Her philosophy is "You can't keep it unless you give it away." When Kia's dad died in 1993, he left her an apartment building, part of which she transformed into a transitional home called WEKhouse (named for William, Elaine, and Kia). The residence, administered under the national umbrella of Oxford House, provides a supportive community for men recovering from drug and alcohol abuse or spousal abuse. For Kia, WEKhouse is a

The Taskmaster: A homeowner husband with a hangdog look emerges from the master bedroom he's redoing. He says Kia strangled him again—the third time that day. Her defense: "I don't take no stuff," she says. "I got on the husband because he wasn't painting right."

Above right: At the Scott Air Force Base near St. Louis, Kia wanted to parachute in to meet her team but had to settle for greeting them from the roof. **Left:** The parachute theme reappears in the family room makeover as curtains at the window. **Above:** Kia slipcovers the sofa outdoors before wrestling it into the house.

natural outgrowth of her upbringing; she remembers how people in need were welcomed into the Dickerson home: "They could always come, have something to eat, get themselves together; then they could move on," says Kia, who has plans for a women's home in the near future.

Another legacy her father left her was his membership in IATSE. He had been the first African American in the union, and Kia didn't want that entrée to the

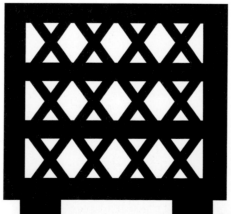

theater business to die with him. So she assumed his membership and started propping for films. "I'm just creating a place and a space for my children and my children's children," says Kia, referring to the broader minority community. "You need to do something to bring people along."

Kia is focused on opening up opportunities for young people. In her design firm, she mentors a graduate design student. When given the opportunity, she speaks at her old high school with this message: "Get educated in whatever it is you like to do. And if the thing you want doesn't exist, then create it for yourself." Kia, the sassy teenager turned sassy adult, has even been inducted into her high school's alumni hall of fame. "I know Sister Verginita turned over in her grave."

Aside from travel, Kia doesn't

before

Challenge: Give this bedroom some romance.
Solution: An Egyptian theme, carried out with
rich colors on the wall and bed and some
fabulous hieroglyph fabric ($69 a yard).

At Kia's House

Home is a stage for the imagination. The theme's the thing.

Every room Kia decorates begins and ends with a theme. Her goal is to fashion a fantasy: a design that goes beyond aesthetic pleasure to mentally and emotionally transport you. "You can paint walls and do very nice draperies and put a throw rug on the floor, but when you do a theme, there's some other stimulation going on," says Kia. "The theatrics—that drama—is stimulating for me."

In Kia's 3,600-square-foot house, each of the 13 rooms is decorated in a different theme: "There's no one style I'm attracted to," says Kia. The powder room and foyer are Egyptian, complete with an 8-foot-high hieroglyphic stone tablet from *Unbreakable*; one guest room is Asian; another guest room is Moroccan; the family room is Caribbean-Afrocentric; the master bedroom is Indian. The Southwestern-style kitchen is about to get an "ode to denim": Kia is covering three existing columns with denim and vintage jean pockets. The valance at top will look like a belt; the molding at bottom will look like a black boot, to which Kia will add spurs. Look for these giant cowboy leg columns to be all the rage.

really have any hobbies other than design-related ones. The woman loves, loves, loves design. The wallpaper store is her social spot. Kia dreams in fully redecorated rooms. Maybe that's why she views her participation on *Trading Spaces* more as a fun extracurricular activity than a moneymaking opportunity. When she was hired, she didn't even realize that the designers got paid. Kia's naïveté seems to run counter to her tough business mind, but designing rooms for people who need some serious help is what she would be doing in her spare time anyway. "For someone to pay you to do what you love, that's the bonus," she says.

Kia treats her current status as a TV personality somewhat casually. Being on *Trading Spaces* isn't the sign of having made it to the top; it's a springboard for aspirations she hasn't even imagined yet.

Above: Kia measures the bed for the wall panel and slipcover while Amy Wynn ponders creating a pair of obelisks to be mounted on each side of the headboard. Other projects include a sprightly ottoman on bun feet and weaving artificial palm leaves into the ceiling fan blades. The leaves looked exotic but interfered with the fan's functioning.

carpentry

Trading Spaces
GMC Accessories

BIG RED MULE

Why?

The rules say "two days, two designers, and one carpenter." But why feature a carpenter? Why not a draper or master upholsterer? Or someone trained to deal with plumbing and electrical problems?

It's because stitching seams and moving outlets will never inspire awe the way the spinning teeth of a table saw do. Because fabric and duct tape are of little help when a diva designer breaks a heel or takes a chunk of wall out along with an unwanted built-in. Because swaggering to push pins into a tiny pin cushion just looks silly compared to the quick draw of a power tool from a heavy, low-slung tool belt holster. And—let's face it—because the two carpenters on *Trading Spaces* can pick up a drill and make it look as sexy as an electric guitar.

But, most of all, because carpenters make it custom. With scraps of lumber, they can build drama into the drabbest of homes—more drama than any designer could create with a $10,000 budget. They've spent three seasons building one TV cabinet after another, yet the *Trading Spaces* carpenters keep surprising viewers by making each piece a true one-of-a-kind. And they accomplish it all while working long days outdoors under the hot sun, through sleet and snow, squinting at designer sketches drawn on coffee shop napkins and magnetic toy doodle boards.

she said he said

Women come up to me and say, "You know, my husband's had a garage full of tools for 25 years, but I've never gone in there and used them because I thought that I couldn't. But I watched you do it, and now I'm like, 'You know what? I can do this.'"

I get just the opposite: The men come up and go, "Hey, man, I've seen that show and, uh, you know, my wife makes me watch it. But I didn't have to do anything for years until that show came on, and now I have to do something every weekend."

The Tricks of the Trade

Don't be fooled. This carpenter crew has a few things up their sleave.

Truth be told, carpenters Amy Wynn Pastor and Ty Pennington have a little help. The *Trading Spaces* trailer is a treasure trove of machines and gadgets— a dream garage on wheels. These carpenters are equipped for anything or at least for trying anything. They have the tools and materials to work up the finest woodcraft details, build chairs out of sheet metal, or fashion table legs from bowling balls. But as more than one designer has learned the hard way, they've yet to drill through solid rock.

They also have Eddie Barnard. Ty and Amy Wynn each film half of the *Trading Spaces* season, but Eddie is a constant on every set. He's their roadie, their assistant, and the one who keeps carpentry projects moving when the head carpenters are stalled by the demands of television. As Ty has often explained, "You're trying to get stuff done and you keep getting called off your projects to film. They're following you around, and you get in such a rush and start making mistakes." Amy Wynn agrees, "We manage it all, but taping takes a lot more time than you might think."

the back

The Trailer

the front

As fast as fast can be—Fast Eddie Barnard

The Fans

Unlike the designers and homeowners working undisturbed inside, the carpenters hammer away surrounded by yellow caution tape and the squeals of a milling crowd. "It's great," says Amy Wynn. "We love it—we really do, but it can be a little distracting. Imagine if you were an accountant and there was a crowd of people around your desk watching you work."

Without fail, the hubbub begins at the nearest home store, the first stop the *Trading Spaces* trailer makes in any town. Spot the moving carpentry shop, and you can be sure the show's carpenters are not far behind. Close on their heels are hordes of eager do-it-yourselfers, who are excited about seeing the trailer—so revved up that a handful of unenlightened, sans-cable shoppers wonder if it's a rock group's tour bus in the parking lot. Ty and Eddie are both pretty great on guitar, but not that great. That's OK, because they'll always be one up on the rock stars: Any room Ty and Eddie trash comes out looking a thousand times better in the end.

amy wynn pastor

Amy Wynn Pastor knows how to play it cool. The dark-haired, dark-eyed natural beauty walks onto a *Trading Spaces* set looking about the same as she does on waking. Swiftly tying up her hair and taking a gulp of lactose-free milk, she's down to work in no time at all. She hustles, but her movements remain slow and easygoing. The stress of another 48-hour crunch can send others into a tizzy, but Amy Wynn responds with sharpened focus.

She's known on-camera as the voice of reason. Viewers often see her listening attentively, nodding and pointing to show a designer that she registers both the design concept and the reasoning behind it. Her own words are clear, concise, and punctuated by a thoughtful pause or a throaty, cut-loose laugh. Whereas Ty, her carpenter compadre, might crack a joke to set trembling homeowners at ease in front of their first power miter saw, Amy Wynn doesn't have to. Her sure gestures alone instill calm and confidence.

Presented with her pragmatic image, Amy Wynn is ready to

Wood: The Natural Choice

Anyone who walks into a room saying "I got some pretty plywood for ya" must have a true passion all for things wood. Amy Wynn explains ...

To describe the joy she's found in a life of carpentry, Amy Wynn points beyond her construction projects to every sensuous aspect of her surroundings. **The Sights.** Forget paint. Amy Wynn prefers to go with the grain for a natural look. **The Sounds.** Nothing is more meditative than the hum of a table saw. "Not that cutting sound," she explains, "but the slow, rising murmur of a machine that's just been turned on." **The Smells.** Cutting into a piece of wood brings out a sudden burst of fragrance; Amy Wynn compares it to "slicing open an orange and watching its juice spurt." **The Splinters.** "I just dig in with my fingernails and pull 'em out," she says. "It hurts, but not as bad as when you press against one still under your skin."

On the set, Amy Wynn happily sports a new T-shirt that reads "Girl With Attitude," then feels compelled to cover it up while making a quick run to a drugstore. "I wore it for working with Gen and Doug. It's my joke with them," she explains. "But in public? That's just rude."

ready to burst. "It's hilarious!" she laughs. "No one who's ever known me would call me the practical one. It is a reality show, and yes, I am that serious on the job, but what you see on TV is only one side of who I am."

The real Amy Wynn is equal parts measure and moxie. Hungry after a morning of intensive yoga, which she practices for health and self-discipline, she can't decide between a choice of salty eggs or sweet French toast. She orders both but eats less than half of each.

Called "Wynn" by her friends, this native Philadelphian gets her strength of character from a classical musician father, a schoolteacher mom, and some forward-thinking Quaker schooling. She grew up playing softball, running around the park with a close-knit group of neighborhood kids, and performing. She was a child actor who hoped for a life on-screen. Little did she know that such a life would also mean keeping up on her tetanus shots.

Her earliest on-camera role was in a commercial that starred her sister as Jane Scoop, reporting from the local house of bargains. Dressed in a mommy-like suit and too-big heels, 5-year-old Amy Wynn pushed a shopping cart and

145

Top row: Working with homeowners in Carpentry World and the finished masterpiece. **Bottom row:** Filming "hay"-larious opener footage down on the farm with designers Doug and Vern.

exclaimed, "I love these prices." In fourth grade, she made herself a peanut butter sandwich in the kitchen of an assumed family while advertising an insurance company. Her mother introduced her to acting before she was old enough to see the opportunity for herself, but it was her will that motivated them to keep finding her new roles. "I loved it," she says. "It was all 'Woooo, we get to leave school and play with other kids on the set!'"

By junior high, Amy Wynn was taking her acting much more seriously than she took her schoolwork. In fact, this get-it-done carpenter wouldn't go near her homework. She confesses, "My grades were horrendous; I'm not proud." The acting that was once her favorite childhood game was now taken away as punishment. Says Amy Wynn, "Those community

playhouse and professional roles were a luxury. I'm grateful my parents cared enough to teach me priorities." While she earned high marks earn in college, but she plodded along through high school classes and eventually found roles in a nearly every school play.

She enrolled as a theatre major at Penn State, but then it happened: Says her former

Who said it was *all* work and no play? Amy Wynn cracks up working with Frank.

professor Mo Stroemel, "We drew her over to the dark side—you know, backstage." To gain an understanding of all that goes into a play, Amy Wynn was required to enroll in classes that dealt with props, sets, and technical direction. But unlike most performance majors, who had that "have to be there" look, Amy Wynn was energetic and enthused. From the first whir of a screw gun in her hands (her first power tool), she was hooked.

147

walls, windows, and furniture for sets. Following her growing passion for carpentry, she soon left acting behind. After college, she took her newfound skills on the road with a traveling Broadway production. She worked as part of a team, always under the time pressure of "the show must go on." Some pieces she made were purely for theatrical illusion, but for structures intended to hold people 18 feet above the stage, her caution and thorough knowledge of construction were essential.

The ironic twist in Amy Wynn's story is that her behind-the-scenes interests landed her a role in front of the camera—on *Trading Spaces*. Her sass didn't hurt either. She worked without a script for her audition tape, smiling wryly as she showed off a table she had modified to fit a new space. She was then as she is now: completely herself on-camera. Although a recent *Makeover Story* episode introduced her as "carpenter and actor," she disagrees. "I'm not acting now. I used to act," she explains.

The only thing that would motivate her to start performing again would be the leading role, perhaps in a vampire movie. Everyone has to have a hobby, and for Amy Wynn it's all things ghoulish. Claiming Halloween as one of her favorite holidays, she penned her first vampire tale as early as kindergarten. During

What's Your A.W.-Q?

Sure, she combines girl-next-door charm with power tool prowess. How well do you know Amy Wynn? Take our quiz and see for yourself!

1. She's "Amy Wynn" and not just "Amy" because

a. Using her middle name was a lot cooler than "Amy P" in a grade school filled with girls named Amy, and afterwards the name just stuck.

b. The extra syllable suits her win-win attitude.

c. This super hot carpenter is just too much woman for one name only.

d. All of the above.

2. Amy Wynn's favorite episode to date was

a. Building four chairs covered entirely in sheet metal.

b. Working in thorny shoulder-high tumbleweeds through a roaring Colorado windstorm.

c. Watching Hildi and Gen tear up flooring, trying to prove that "a bedroom really can look like a patio."

d. None of the above.

3. Amy Wynn dreams of having time to build

a. Playgrounds across the country for Habitat for Humanity.

b. Shelves for her very own workroom.

c. A love shack for her and Douglas Wilson.

d. A and B but never C.

4. Besides rubber mallets, Amy Wynn has demolished built-in cabinets with

a. Her fists.

b. Her feet.

c. Gen's feet.

d. All of the above.

5. Amy Wynn has built pieces for designers who

a. Scribble sketches onto the palm of her hand (ahem, Gen).

b. Provide measurements as helpful as "the length of one fat man with arms extended" (Attaway, Frank!).

c. Expect shelving units completed at the end of Day 2 but don't factor in any time for two coats of paint to dry prior to the big Reveal.

d. A and B but (oops! Time flies in New Orleans!) not C. Oh well, she's close enough to perfect.

ANSWERS: D, D, D, D, and D.

From the Hip

What exactly does Amy Wynn keep in that tool belt of hers? Not a hammer (it's too darn heavy and limits her movement). She carries only a few basic tools, and these are her favorites:

Pocket Square	A small metal triangle with lots of angle markings, useful in laying out cuts or as a guide for her circular saw.
Carpenter's Pencil	A wide, flat pencil that won't roll off the workbench.
Nail Set	A steel punch that looks a little like a pencil without lead. It's used to countersink a nailhead, driving the nail below the surface of the wood so the hole can be filled and finished.
Lip Gloss	So essential, it has a specially dedicated pocket in her tool belt. The gloss keeps her pretty, yes, but also protects her lips from chapping in the wind or other harsh weather.

Halloween as one of her favorite holiday, she penned her first vampire tale as early as kindergarten. During a high school family history project, she learned with a thrill that the grandfather she was named for ("Wynn" is short for William) had migrated from Transylvania.

As for her own decorating preferences, Amy Wynn's home is a cozy and often empty apartment. She's proud of her bedroom, which includes some inherited pieces and a restful neutral palette, but the rest is no design showcase and in fact includes her worst carpentry effort ever—teetering bathroom shelves spontaneously slapped together one afternoon with nothing but a hammer and a handheld saw. Noting these primitive shelves, she says with regret, "All those great tools I have on the show? They keep

149

Above: You "otter" get to know her! Animal lover Amy Wynn gets a feisty sea otter to perform a few tricks for the camera during a visit to SeaWorld.

amy wynn pastor

Born: May 9, 1976
Hometown: Philadelphia, Ponnsylvania
Favorite Saying: "I'm all over that!"
First Loves: James Dean and her teddy bear David
Fun Night Out: Cooing over infant nephew or watching
a good football game
Photographed in Philadelphia, Pennsylvania on November 9, 2002

hopes, when time permits, to find herself a house with a workroom where she can use them. She stores notes and drawings of pieces she'd like to build someday, the first of which is a Noah's ark with portholes large enough to show off her nephew's stuffed animals. She'd also like to duplicate and keep for herself the smooth butcher-block-top kitchen table she made for one of Genevieve's Long Island homeowners.

Amy Wynn is single, which adds a fiery dimension to her fan base. For the record, those tight clothes she wears are a matter of safety, not sex appeal. (She had her closest call when a loose fleece pullover got caught up in a machine.) However, she intentionally chose a slinky gold number to wear to last year's Emmys. "That dress was made for Jennifer Lopez," she says, "but I got it!"

Bad carpenter come-on lines aside, Amy Wynn doesn't mind being appreciated physically. After all, she had posters of TV stars on her own walls as a teen. Her greatest satisfaction comes from hearing comments from female viewers who feel empowered by her example. Says Amy Wynn, "Little girls are telling me that they want to grow up and be a carpenter. How cool is that?"

Amy Wynn, M.D. When decorating emergencies arise, Amy Wynn rushes in the doctor's bag.

"It's a black tool bag really," explains Amy Wynn. "I just call it that. You know, how doctors always have something to grab and carry when someone needs help fast." In her emergency bag are chisels, socket wrenches, a pry bar, a hammer, and a big mallet (useful for whacking something that doesn't fit into place or for dealing with temperamental designers). The bag also holds her raincoat, her bug spray, moisturizer for her hands, and—until she runs out—extra pencils and a second tape measure. These last extras aren't merely the compulsive additions of a superorganized gal; Amy Wynn confesses, "I lose everything."

Build it and they will come.

Custom-Built by Wynn

Sure, she's the gal on the *Trading Spaces* set who can wrangle a jigsaw or skillfully aim a nail gun, but most fans aren't aware of Amy Wynn's design contributions to the show:

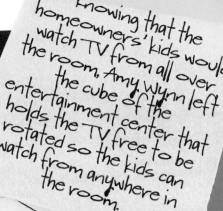

Knowing that the homeowners' kids would watch TV from all over the room, Amy Wynn left the cube of the entertainment center that holds the TV free to be rotated so the kids can watch from anywhere in the room.

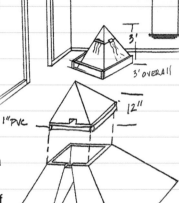

Indiana: River Valley Road Gen asked Amy Wynn for a "Danish Modern-like" entertainment center that wasn't centered to use in a kid-friendly Indiana family room. Wynn worked with Gen's original request, then came back to the designer at 9 p.m. on Day I with the idea for this sleek, playful television/toy storage unit and stackable cubes, featuring extra stackers that double as fun side tables.

Indianapolis: Halleck Way The pharaohs had a little more help than Amy Wynn, but that didn't stop her from trying to re-create one of the Seven Wonders of the Ancient World. She built a fountain frame for Kia's Egyptian-theme room, making it in the shape of the Great Pyramid of Khufu at Giza. But Kia's team couldn't waterproof the structure, and after it spouted more water than what seemed like the Nile, they decided to throw in the towel.

Frank wanted a castle headboard with three tiers topped with finials of a sun, moon, and star. Wynn finished in time to note the homeowners' obsession for their dog and build a matching bed for the pup.

Jackson: Gold Pond Amy Wynn had never built a chaise lounge, but that didn't stop Laurie from asking for one. Designers aren't used to drawing up plans for structurally demanding pieces such as chairs, so that left a lot up to Wynn. Her only instructions were to spend as little as possible and make it look expensive. Knowing Laurie, Wynn also knew the design needed to be lean and classic, with a clean profile. She constructed the chaise for a ridiculously low $65, using manufactured wood and covering all edges with an oak veneer that took a nice stain. Laurie made Wynn's design roar, covering it in a minimalistic animal print.

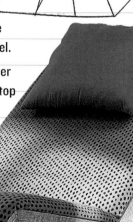

ty pennington

> **There are so many houses we have yet to destroy.**

Shoots where Ty is on the set have their own special rhythm. They begin with a few teenage girls from the neighborhood spotting the *Trading Spaces* trailer on their block and begging their parents to let them stay home from school. After the school bus leaves, their moms, embarrassed by their own gawking, swing by under the pretense of entertaining their toddlers, who thankfully always find a way to stay fascinated. The teen girls return after school, freshly primped. They bring their friends. Then their mothers return, primped as well, along with their own friends. Sometimes grandmothers show up to get a glimpse. Guys are in the mix too, lost in the excitement and the estrogen. By nightfall, family, friends, neighbors, and strangers begin vying with each other for position along the barrier of yellow caution tape to Ty Land.

"It's getting pretty *Tiger Beat*," Ty has been known to say. The talented carpenter with a wit as sharp as his carved abs does his best to take it all in stride. Asked for an autograph by a 15-year-old girl in a home store, he turned the tables on her,

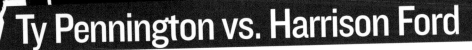

Ty Pennington vs. Harrison Ford

What does the resident hunk on *Trading Spaces* have in common with film legend Harrison Ford?

Harrison Ford	Ty Pennington
Successful Carpenter turned Leading Man	Successful Carpenter and Aspiring Actor
Attracts with the grave charisma of film legends Cooper and Fonda	Lives in the same city as Jane Fonda
Pals around with the tall, furry Chewbacca as Han Solo in *Star Wars*	Pals around with short, furry Frank as the solo handyman on *Trading Spaces*
Had a bit role in *Apocalypse Now*	Has a great collection of drill bits
Dived 250 feet into canyon waters to save the day in *The Fugitive*	Dove 2 feet into trash bins looking for scrap wood to save a budget-strapped Doug
Made women swoon as action-adventure-archaeologist Indiana Jones	Makes women swoon, period

154

Asked for an autograph by a 15-year-old girl in a home improvement store, he turned the tables on her, signing, "You're totally hot. Love, Ty Pennington." Her response? "You're really silly."

signing, "You're totally hot. Love, Ty Pennington." Her response? "You're really silly." He is, really, except about his craft.

Ty is the carpenter most likely to turn home makeovers into an extreme sport. He's been seen wheeling down a driveway on Frank's ottoman, surfing on Kia's hanging bed, and diving into trash bins to uncover scrap lumber for a table for Doug. He's cute and troublesome, like a boy you love to watch misbehave. Frank has described him as "a little sprite. Like a gnome looking for a mushroom." Whereas Amy Wynn

tries logic when she has to negotiate projects with the designers, Ty teases them into submission—or tries to.

Sometimes his will can appear a little strong. He's quick to question directions and offer up his own solutions. "That's great, but I have a better idea." is the way it comes out on-camera. Viewers might hear pushiness or even cockiness in that comment, but that's not the way cast and crew see it. They trust Ty's abilities and know he has valuable things to say. Look past the 'tude, the thrift store duds, and the hair that's carefully coiffed to look as if he doesn't care, and you can see that Ty does care, a lot.

155

You can identify Ty's home by the peach surfboard leaning outside his front door. The house is a Victorian bungalow, full of history in the architectural details but furnished with a modern mix of '60s swank and primitives.

He takes his carpentry seriously, and his design even more so. For Ty it's not enough to get the job done. Designer Genevieve Gorder adds, "Ty's not just a great carpenter. He's an excellent designer as well, with an eye for color. That guy could build me a world." Maybe Gen would be safer with Hildi or Kia, because Ty's latest fascination is the Dutch Droog Design, which recently transformed manure into bulb planters. He's boasted, "They're making great stuff out of s@#%. My kind of heroes."

Born and raised in Atlanta, Ty learned woodworking from his father. Ty spent his early years romping around the urban Brookhaven neighborhood, then fell into despair after his family moved to the burbs in Marietta. That was in the late '70s, when everyone else in America made the same trek, leaving buses behind for car pools. Ty hated being driven around at first, but from the looks of his big splurge, a '65 Mercury Comet, he seems to have made his peace with car culture. Country star Travis Tritt was one of Ty's neighbors, which says something about Ty's mix of urban attitude and strong Southern roots.

Ty earned a degree in graphic design at The Art Institute of Atlanta. He used his carpentry skills to help pay for his education. He had a passion for the fine arts as well, so after graduating, he continued to work days

What's your Ty-Q?

If you're like most of America, you want to get to know the guy behind the Ty. Take this quiz and find out more about the *Trading Spaces* carpenter who's used wood glue as a skin moisturizer.

1. "Ty" is short for
a. Tyrone, after the swashbuckling hunk of classic film, Tyrone Power
b. Tyler, after the 10th President of the United States, who later became a rebel statesman of the Southern Confederacy
c. TaeBo, which he uses in defense against pushy designers
d. Tygert (no joke)

2. Ty has gallantly rushed to the rescue of
a. Designers without finished drawings
b. Kia from the possible crash of her Taj Mahal colonnades and suspended "magic carpet" bed
c. Frank, from himself
d. A and B but sadly, not C

3. Ty is still trying to forget
a. Building a platform bed for Hildi out of rock-hard Brazilian cherry wood
b. Watching Doug construct a headboard for a 12-year-old boy out of branches found on the side of the road—in chigger country
c. Goofing off on a ladder and dropping his drill on the glass globe of Frank's $250 ceiling fan
d. None of the above

4. After-hours, off the set, you can catch Ty
a. Playing rockin' acoustic guitar with assistant known as "Fast Eddie"
b. Drawing pictures of his friends as animals (Doug makes a cute lizard.)
c. Boogie-boarding on a homeowner's rolling ottoman
d. Any one of the above and much more

5. Hunky Ty imagines his true love match as
a. Grace Kelly
b. Ten centerfolds and one jealous Hildi
c. Wendy from *Peter Pan*
d. His live-in girlfriend of four years (Sorry!)

6. 9 out of 10 fans agree— Ty's best feature is
a. His soulful eyes
b. His rock-hard abs
c. His moppish yet spikey hair
d. Okay, even this quiz is becoming a bit too *Tiger Beat* for its own good!

ANSWERS: D, D, D, D, and D.

ty pennington

Raised: Atlanta, Georgia
Hometown: Atlanta, Georgia
Favorite Pastime: Surfing, skateboarding, and sarcasm
Artistic Heroes: Marlon Brando, *Naked* author David Sedaris
Most Revealing Quote: "I scare myself, more than you know."
Pet Project: Writing his how-to book, to be published by Hyperion

> **One way to create space is to take things low to the ground. Especially if you have low ceilings. You can create a lot more space in the room by reducing the height of a table or bed.**

as a carpenter and attended night classes in painting and sculpture at the Atlanta College of Art. Later he combined his skills to work as a set designer, painting sets for the movie *Leaving Las Vegas*. He still paints today.

But it didn't take long for others to figure out that Ty's chiseled cheeks were a work of art themselves. After college, Ty signed with a New York modeling agency. Assignments for J.Crew, Swatch, Body Glove, and Sprite took him across the globe. He did TV spots too, striking poses for Diet Coke, Macy's, and Levi's. Maybe that's where he caught the acting bug. Ty's not afraid of the spotlight and loves to ham it up. "I'm the kid who never grows up," he's explained to fans. "I want to have fun my entire life."

He's off to a good start on that goal: He's a surfer, an avid skateboarder, and a soccer player. He plays guitar (he has a dozen of them) and recently cut a CD (entitled *Thick and Vainy*) with his local Atlanta band. On the road with *Trading Spaces*, he keeps his musical ear in tune by playing acoustic guitar with assistant carpenter Eddie. It's a good way to spend long nights in hotel rooms and a great release after a long workday.

Ty used his modeling income to buy a former piano factory in Atlanta in 1996. He converted the factory into seven loft apartments, and the leftover piano parts he discovered in the process found their way into a few of his sculptures. After completing the

He Said, She Said

Amy Wynn and Ty level with us and share what it's really like to work in front of and behind the cameras with cable TV's most daring designers.

Ty on Hildi: "She goes beyond boundaries to make sure she's doing stuff nobody else has done. You've got to give her points for that. I'm hoping we'll go into fur."

Ty on Doug: "He changes plans midway through. I'll start out building a table, and he'll turn it into a door."

Ty on Laurie: "She's the sweetest thing, but she'll spend all her money on drapes and chandeliers, then ask me to build an entertainment center for $80... not real aware of the price of lumber these days."

Ty on Vern: "He expects a lot. You need to have your best game on with Vern, because he's determined to make it look more like $10,000."

Amy Wynn on Genevieve: "So much fun to work with, and so creative. You can't help but get drawn into her little fantasy world where everything is fun and colorful and exciting. I also appreciate her 'nature-y' side. She respects wood like I do."

Amy Wynn on Edward: "He's such a sweet gentleman and very open-minded. He'll come with all the specifics like Vern but then let me get creative like Frank."

Amy Wynn on Frank: "He says 'give me a bench this long' and trusts that I'll come up with something he'll like. It's always fun getting creative with him."

Amy Wynn on Kia: "She has a background where she's used to building things herself, so she can have a harder time letting go. She's really into talking about the details. And she walks out to check on me a lot."

lofts, he formed his own business renovating homes and building furniture. Today he runs F.U. (Furniture Unlimited), his own custom design shop in Atlanta, but he doesn't always have time to do all the work himself. "I design the pieces," Ty explains to his customers, "but my partner and a team of guys build my stuff."

You can tell Ty's own place by the peach surfboard leaning outside his front door. The house is a Victorian bungalow, full of historical details but furnished with a modern mix of '60s swank and primitives. The carpenter with the droopy pants likes a neat look, without clutter. That's not an easy look to achieve in

an old home, where rooms aren't as large as their counterparts in newer houses. Ty has his tricks. He's offered some of these tips to fans, including this: "One way to create space is to take things low to the ground, especially if you have low ceilings. You can create a lot more space in the room by reducing the height of a table or bed."

Smart and handsome to boot—too bad he's taken. Ty shares his home with his girlfriend of four years. "Who else would have me?" he's been known to joke. Is he kidding? Who wouldn't want a handsome handy guy around the house?

episode guide

Think you're the ultimate *Trading Spaces* fan? Prove it by rating the room redos of every episode of the show in this handy-dandy listing guide.

This complete, chronological tour through the years with your favorite decorating show is so chock-full of facts, figures, and funnies that even die-hard fans will learn a thing or two! Check out the Icon Legend on below to help locate episodes with Designer Diva Fits, Tearjerker Reactions, and more. And don't forget to record your opinion of each and every transformation by using the super-easy ☺ ☺ ☹ Smiley-Face scale.

💣 = Demolition   ☹ = Tearjerker   ✳ = Ceiling Fan   😈 = Diva Fit   🔌 = Homeowners with Power Tools

◄▋ = Paint Explosion   ⑦ = What Were They Thinking?   ⚒ = Carpenter to the Rescue $ = Budget Crisis   ♥ = Fan Favorite

Season 1

Knoxville: Fourth & Gill

Cast: Alex, Frank, Laurie, Amy Wynn

The Rooms: In the premiere episode, Frank brightens a den by using a faux-suede finish in shades of gold on the walls, reupholstering the homeowners' Arts and Crafts furniture, and painting two armoires in shades of red, gold, and black. Laurie punches up a bland kitchen by painting the walls electric pear, retiling the floor in large black and white checks, and using chrome accents. She also creates an organized family message and filing center.

Watch For: Frank demonstrates the "Frank Droop," meant to keep your arm from getting tired while painting. (It's a shoulder shimmy crossed with a slight back bend.)

Budget Note: Both Frank and Laurie are under budget, but host Alex never even mentions the fact during the end Designer Chat segment.

Frank's Room: ☺ ☺ ☹
Laurie's Room: ☺ ☺ ☹

Knoxville: Forest Glen ☹ 😈

Cast: Alex, Doug, Hildi, Amy Wynn

The Rooms: Doug creates a romantic bedroom, which he titles "Country Urbane," by painting the walls sage green, building an upholstered bed, pickling an existing vanity, and making a privacy screen. Hildi designs a sleek living room, painting the walls a dark putty, sewing white slipcovers and curtains, hanging spotlights on the walls to showcase the homeowners' art, and building end tables that spin on lazy Susans.

Fashion Report: Doug wears dark, angular glasses and has curly hair.

Notable: On his first episode, Doug throws a couple of low-voltage diva fits: one in which he paces and repeatedly mumbles "Why stress tomorrow when you can stress today?" and another in which he walks off-camera and screams.

Crisis: Hildi creates controversy by wanting to paint a thin black stripe around the edge of the wood floor. Her homeowners hate the idea and refuse to take any part in it. She and Alex eventually do it.

Reveal-ing Moment: One of the living room homeowners starts to cry unhappy tears and exclaims, "Oh my God! They painted my floor!"

Doug's Room: ☺ ☺ ☹
Hildi's Room: ☺ ☺ ☹

Athens: County Road ☹ ✳

Cast: Alex, Frank, Hildi, Amy Wynn

The Rooms: Frank brightens a child's room by painting the walls lavender, hanging a swing from the ceiling, making a wall-size art area with chalkboard spray paint, and spray-painting a mural of white trees. Hildi updates a kitchen/living room area by painting the dark wood paneling and ceiling ecru, hanging cream draperies, slipcovering chairs with monkey-print fabric, building shelves to showcase the homeowners' pewter collection, and painting several pieces of furniture black.

Safety First: When Frank's female homeowner won't tie her hair back while spackling, he tells her that his hair is gone because of a bad spackling incident.

Age Matters: Frank is preoccupied with youth in this episode, noting that he's "a 5-year-old kid with chest hair." Later, while dealing with a nagging Alex: "Are you sure you aren't a reincarnated 2-year-old?"

Hurry Up!: Frank falls way behind on Day 2, so Alex takes the AlexCam to a retirement community and gets shots of seniors saying that they've heard Frank might not finish on time.

Quotable Quote: One of Hildi's homeowners must not know her very well; she tells Hildi, "You could've lived in pioneer times."

Frank's Room: ☺ ☺ ☹
Hildi's Room: ☺ ☺ ☹

Alpharetta: Providence Oaks

Cast: Alex, Hildi, Roderick, Amy Wynn

The Rooms: Hildi re-creates a dining room using the existing dining table, aubergine paint, pistachio curtains, two-tone slipcovers, a striking star-shape light fixture, and a privacy screen. Roderick brightens a den/guest room by painting off-white stripes on the existing khaki walls, stenciling a sun motif in a deep rust-red, slipcovering the furniture with an off-white fabric, and installing a wall-length

desk that can be hidden with curtains.

Yucky Moment: Amy Wynn holds a pencil between her toes while measuring out the desk unit with Roderick.

Time Waster: Hildi, Alex, and Hildi's homeowners search for two days to find china—digging in the attic and asking the other homeowners where they store it—so they can set the table for the end shot. They never find it.

Notable: Although he's never seen again on the show, Roderick is the first designer to use the term "homework" while talking to the homeowners about what needs to be done before the next morning. However, this is not the standard "homework assignment" scene that appears in later episodes.

Hildi's Room: ☺ ☺ ☹
Roderick's Room: ☺ ☺ ☹

Lawrenceville: Pine Lane 💣 ✳ 🔌 ☹

Cast: Alex, Dez, Hildi, Amy Wynn

The Rooms: Dez adds a feminine touch to a dark wood-paneled living room by whitewashing the walls, painting the fireplace, and dismantling a banister. She finds new ways to display the husband's taxidermy and decoy duck collection, including creating a custom duck lamp. Hildi brings the outdoors in, creating an organically hip living room with a tree limb valance, wicker furniture, minty-white walls, and an armoire covered with dried leaves.

Paint Problems: Dez says that she hasn't painted a room herself in 20 years—not since she was a "starving artist"—and severely underestimates how long the project will take. By the end of the day, she is covered in paint—unusual for a designer on the show. Also, Dez's paint problems are complicated by one of her homeowners who apparently spends both days priming and painting one built-in bookcase. His excuse: "Paint dries on its own time."

Wonder Woman: Amy Wynn demolishes Dez's banister seemingly with her bare hands.

Fashion Report: Hildi wears flats! Dez wears a strange little hat during her Designer Chat.

Notable: Hildi offers a tired Dez some advice at the end of Day I: "Delegate, delegate, delegate."

Dez's Room: ☺ ☺ ☹
Hildi's Room: ☺ ☺ ☹

Buckhead: Canter Road

Cast: Alex, Genevieve, Laurie, Amy Wynn

The Rooms: Gen gets wild in a kitchen by painting the walls electric pear, adding silver accents, using colanders as light covers, and removing cabinet doors. Laurie creates a crisp living room by painting the walls chocolate brown, laying a sea-grass rug, and adding cream and white slipcovers and curtains.

Fashion Report: Gen is barefoot the entire episode.

Quotable Quote: Gen wants to change the flooring but doesn't have time. She expresses her disappointment by saying, "Linoleum bites."

Notable: The now famous "Carpenter Consult" scene debuts, with Laurie consulting Amy Wynn.

Gen's Room: ☺ 😐 ☹
Laurie's Room: ☺ 😐 ☹

Washington, DC: Cleveland Park

Cast: Alex, Dez, Doug, Ty

The Rooms: Dez creates a funky-festive living room by combining electric pear, white, gray, black, and red paint in solids, stripes, polka dots, and textured faux finishes. Doug goes retro in a basement by making a beanbag sofa and a kidney-shape coffee table and painting the walls bright orange.

Scary Project: Dez creates a custom "Medusa lamp" featuring three heads, spiky lightbulbs, and Christmas lights.

Notable: One of Dez's young female homeowners is smitten with Ty and quickly volunteers to work with him on a project, leaving the remaining partner to say to Dez, "Who does she think she's kidding?"

Budget Crunch: Claiming he doesn't have enough money to buy legs for his coffee table, Doug substitutes plastic tumblers filled with plaster of Paris.

Quotable Quote: One of Doug's homeowners criticizes Doug's free-form planning by saying, "I wish you spent as much time laying this project out as you did on your hair this morning."

Dez's Room: ☺ 😐 ☹
Doug's Room: ☺ 😐 ☹

Alexandria: Riefton Court

Cast: Alex, Frank, Genevieve, Ty

The Rooms: Frank cozies a country kitchen by creating a picket-fence shelving unit and using seven pastel paint colors to create a hand-painted quilt. Gen goes graphic in a living room, blowing up and recropping family photos, turning an existing entertainment center on its side, and painting the walls bright red.

Quotable Quote: Explaining his design, Frank says, "I thought…country quilt. This looks like a quilt threw up in here, but when you see the result, you're gonna love it."

Conflict: Frank questions why Ty is spending more time on Gen's project and less time on the "quilt": "Could it be because [at] the other house the individual is very tall, very gorgeous, and has enough sex appeal to knock over a troupe?"

Oops!: While drilling into the entertainment center, Gen talks about how soft the wood is yet still manages to break her drill bit in it.

Frank's Room: ☺ 😐 ☹
Gen's Room: ☺ 😐 ☹

Annapolis: Fox Hollow

Cast: Alex, Genevieve, Laurie, Ty

The Rooms: Gen warms a living room with butterscotch paint, white curtains, framed family pictures, and a combination wood/carpet floor. Laurie cleans a drab kitchen with muted pumpkin paint, new light fixtures, and a custom pot hanger.

Coincidence?: The paint colors that Gen and Laurie choose—butterscotch and muted pumpkin—are incredibly

---

similar despite the different names.

Notable: Gen leads morning stretches with her homeowners before getting to work on Day 2. Laurie removes her first ceiling fan on the show.

Gen's Room: ☺ 😐 ☹
Laurie's Room: ☺ 😐 ☹

Philadelphia: Strathmore Road

Cast: Alex, Frank, Dez, Amy Wynn

The Rooms: Frank goes earthy by painting a living room brown with a sueding technique. He also creates a window seat with storage, handmade accents, and a child-size tepee. Dez tries for "casual elegance" in a living room, using purple paint, a repeated gray harlequin pattern on the walls, and an end table lamp made out of a trash can.

Quotable Quotes: Frank trying to figure out how comfortable a cushion is: "What's the heinie quotient on that?" Frank running out of time on Day 2: "I'm so tense…you could literally use me as a paper press."

Fashion Report: In her Designer Chat, Dez wears a pointy diamond-shape hat.

Oops!: Frank is 23 cents over budget.

Reveal-ing Moment: The homeowners hate Dez's room with a vengeance, stating "We've got the set of *The Dating Game* on our walls" and "Beetlejuice lives here."

Frank's Room: ☺ 😐 ☹
Dez's Room: ☺ 😐 ☹

Philadelphia: Valley Road

Cast: Alex, Doug, Laurie, Amy Wynn

The Rooms: Doug softens a sunroom he names "Blue Lagoon" by painting the walls a deep robin's egg blue, painting blue and white diamonds on the hardwood floor, hanging whitewashed bamboo blinds, and adding pale yellow accents. He adds a *Rear Window* touch by placing a pair of binoculars (which he finds in the basement) in the sunroom so the homeowners can watch their children playing outside. Laurie goes Greek, painting a living room deep russet with black and white accents, adding white Grecian urns, and even creating a white bust using one of her homeowners as a model.

Yucky Moment: Doug uses picture wire as dental floss.

Notable: Laurie thinks she's so ahead of schedule on Day 1 that she leads Doug to believe she's been asked to slow down and relax with the family dog so as not to finish too early. She then falls quite behind on Day 2 and becomes very stressed about finishing.

Doug's Room: ☺ 😐 ☹
Laurie's Room: ☺ 😐 ☹

Philadelphia: Galahad Road

Cast: Alex, Hildi, Genevieve, Amy Wynn

The Rooms: Hildi warms a family-friendly living/dining room by introducing coffee-color walls, a midnight blue fireplace, a custom-built sectional couch, and zebra-stripe dining chair covers. Gen brightens a basement den by painting the walls lily pad green, adding orange accents, installing a white modern couch, and weaving white fabric on the ceiling to cover the drop-ceiling tiles.

Conflict: Hildi's homeowners are doubtful that their neighbors will like their new room; they fight her on most decisions.

Fashion Report: Gen wears a cowboy hat the entire episode.

Wise Wynn: Gen plans to demolish an entire wall, but Amy Wynn talks her out of it due to structural concerns.

Wicked Wynn: Amy Wynn tells Alex that the coffee table she's constructing for Gen is "really, really ugly" and that she'd throw it out if it were in her room.

Hildi's Room: ☺ 😐 ☹
Gen's Room: ☺ 😐 ☹

Knoxville: Courtney Oak

Cast: Alex, Frank, Laurie, Amy Wynn

The Rooms: Frank gets in touch with his "inner child" by painting the walls of a basement light denim blue, free-handing murals of trees and flowers, and spray-painting fluffy white clouds. Laurie goes organic by painting a bedroom a deep pistachio green, adding soft draperies, painting a vine around the vanity mirror, and using a cornice board to drape fabric on either side of the headboard.

Fan Debates: Laurie removes another ceiling fan. Alex argues with Frank about his decision to leave two brown ceiling fans in place. Frank defends his choice: "With people dying everywhere and starving children, really, two ceiling fans of the wrong color are minor trivialities."

Quotable Quotes: Frank to Alex: "I would never beat you. You're a nice person, even though you ask some pointed and completely ugly questions."

Notable: Laurie moves closer to that superstressed Southern belle image that viewers know and love.

Frank's Room: ☺ 😐 ☹
Laurie's Room: ☺ 😐 ☹

163

Cincinnati: Melrose Avenue

Cast: Alex, Hildi, Frank, Ty

The Rooms: Frank adds soft, Victorian touches to a living room by exposing the existing wood floor, creating a faux-tin fireplace surround, painting a navy wall border with a rose motif, creating a fireplace screen that matches the border, and building a bench-style coffee table. Hildi gets crafty in a kitchen, creating her own wallpaper with tissue paper and flower stencils based on a fabric pattern. She installs a found dishwasher, extends the countertop, builds an island out of the kitchen table, paints the ceiling and the furniture yellow, and lays vinyl tile flooring.

Love Connection?: Frank's male and female homeowners admit to crushes on Alex and Ty, respectively.

Notable: Frank admits to country-and-western dancing with his wife.

Hildi's Room: ☺ 😐 ☹
Frank's Room: ☺ 😐 ☹

Cincinnati: Sturbridge Road ☹

Cast: Alex, Genevieve, Doug, Ty

The Rooms: Gen creates an Indian bedroom for a teenage girl by painting the walls with warm golden and red tones, hanging a beaded curtain, and creating a draped canopy. Doug turns a dining room into a "Zen-Buddhist-Asian room" with a chocolate brown ceiling, warm honey-copper walls, randomly placed Venetian plaster squares, and folded-metal-screen window treatments.

Fashion Report: Gen and her homeowners wear Indian forehead markings on both days for inspiration.

Quotable Quote: Gen calls Doug a "weasel" for usurping some of her lumber and states, "I think he's feeling insecure about his room or he's got a little crush on me and he's just really sad about the rejection."

Scary Stuff: Doug raps.

Notable: Doug gives the first official homework assignment on the show.

Gen's Room: ☺ 😐 ☹
Doug's Room: ☺ 😐 ☹

Cincinnati: Madison & Forest ☹

Cast: Alex, Doug, Laurie, Ty

The Rooms: Doug transforms a Victorian living room into an industrial loft with multiple shades of purple paint, a yellow ceiling, custom art made from coordinating paint chips, wall sconces made of candy dishes, and a chair reupholstered in Holstein fabric. Laurie warms a tiny bedroom with mustard yellow paint, a custom-built entertainment center, and a short suspended bed canopy.

Yucky Moment: Doug rips out old carpet but isn't happy with the smell, calling it "eau de cat."

Tensions: Marital tension between Doug's homeowners rises to the surface on Day 2. Doug and Ty get into a huff as well while building a custom mirror that's too big to fit above the fireplace.

Hurry Up!: Doug has his homeowners create art projects in a 10-minute time frame. Alex walks around with a stopwatch.

Notable: This is the first episode in which both designers make a point of assigning homework and leaving for the evening.

Doug's Room: ☺ 😐 ☹
Laurie's Room: ☺ 😐 ☹

San Diego: Elm Ridge   ♥

Cast: Alex, Genevieve, Hildi, Amy Wynn

The Rooms: In this infamous episode, Gen truly brings the outdoors in: She covers a bedroom wall with Oregon moss, lays a natural-tone tile floor, and adds a canopy that is lit from above with twinkling lights. Hildi works to convince her homeowners that they can brighten a bedroom by painting the walls and furniture black, adding zebra-stripe floor cubes, and using exposed subflooring in place of carpet.

Un-bear-able: One of Gen's male homeowners constantly carries around a teddy bear, setting the bear in various places throughout the project.

Yucky Moment: One of Gen's homeowners complains that the moss wall "smells like somebody's old underwear."

Tile Hell: Due to time constraints, Gen chooses to lay floor tiles with liquid nails instead of adhesive and grout. Her team ends up re-laying many tiles during Day 2 because the adhesive doesn't quite work. Hildi's grout unexpectedly dries white and looks terrible next to dark concrete tiles. Hildi improvises by knowingly going over budget to buy rugs. Bonus: Hildi drives off in a sporty silver convertible for her emergency shopping trip.

Busted: Hildi creates a copper mesh bust using herself as a model. The female homeowner isn't thrilled with the idea and says, "You went to design school?"

Notable: The moss wall homeowners actually like Gen's design well enough.

Gen's Room: ☺ 😐 ☹
Hildi's Room: ☺ 😐 ☹

San Diego: Hermes Avenue

Cast: Alex, Laurie, Genevieve, Amy Wynn

The Rooms: Laurie brightens a kitchen by painting the walls Tiffany-box blue, installing a wooden slat grid system on one wall, hanging butter yellow draperies, building a banquette seating area, coating the stove in chrome-colored paint, and painting the cabinets butter yellow. Gen uses Georgia O'Keeffe's Southwestern paintings as inspiration for transforming a living room. She paints the walls clay red, hangs a cow skull above the fireplace, adds a woven rug, hangs new light fixtures, frames large black and white cropped photos of the homeowners' children, builds a distressed coffee table with firewood legs, and covers the existing baby bumpers with crafts fur.

Oops!: Gen accidentally steps into a bucket full of spackling compound and must hop around on one foot until one of her homeowners brings her a towel.

Conflict: Laurie wants all of her carpentry projects completed by the end of Day 1; Amy Wynn becomes testy and tells her no.

Resourceful: Laurie reframes a wide, off-center window by covering it with a larger, centered wood frame and nailing bamboo place mats to the frame to cover the window like blinds.

Budget Buster: Laurie can't afford to spend money on cabinet hardware, so her homeowners ask for permission to

buy it themselves as a gift for their friends. Laurie agrees. During Designer Chat, Alex says that she'll bend the rules once for Laurie, but never again.

Reveal-ing Moment: The female living room homeowner is so excited about her room that she picks up Alex—twice.

Laurie's Room: ☺ 😐 ☹
Gen's Room: ☺ 😐 ☹

San Diego: Wilbur Street

Cast: Alex, Frank, Doug, Amy Wynn

The Rooms: Frank mixes British Colonial and tropical looks in a living room using soft mauve paint, exposed wood flooring, several flowerpots and vases, and a custom architectural piece. Doug updates a dark kitchen with a "Tuscan Today" theme, using Venetian plaster tinted "Tuscan Mango" (OK, it's orange), painting the cabinets white and orange, and installing wood flooring.

Quotable Quotes: Frank-isms abound in this episode. Frank on his wall hanging: "OK, now we're gonna make a metal taco." Frank on how tired he feels: "If someone invited me out to dinner, I'd have to hire someone to chew my food." And Frank on his finished room: "You could get malaria in this room it's so tropical."

Oops!: Frank originally wants to install a parquet floor with 4×4-inch squares. Amy Wynn cuts several squares, but they only cover one-eighth of the floor. Amy has to stop cutting because the saw burns out. Doug winds up going to buy prefab flooring.

Ouch!: Alex helps Frank hot-glue moss to flowerpots and manages to lay her entire palm on a freshly glued spot. She gets hot glue and moss stuck to her hand, and Frank runs off to find first aid.

Frank's Room: ☺ 😐 ☹
Doug's Room: ☺ 😐 ☹

Knoxville: Stubbs Bluff

Cast: Alex, Frank, Doug, Ty

The Rooms: Doug brings a farmhouse kitchen up-to-date by painting the walls a muted coffee color, adding sage and lilac accents, building benches in the dining area, painting the cabinets, and laying vinyl tile. Frank lets the ideas flow while punching up a basement with a karaoke stage, a tiki hut bar, and several other tropical accents—including a canoe for seating.

Oops!: Even though Doug and Alex spend much of the episode mixing plaster to coat a shovel and a pitchfork to hang on the wall, the plaster won't dry fast enough, so Doug ends up spray-painting the tools instead.

Fashion Report: Frank wears a hula outfit—complete with coconut bra—and asks, "Am I showing too much cleavage? Be honest."

Quotable Quotes: Frank disses Ty's mellow attitude, saying "He goes through like life's little pixie, like a little gnome looking for a mushroom." While explaining a crafts project to Alex, Frank suggests she make hers look like "you just went to the jungle and knocked over a monkey and dug up the soil and put it on a pot."

Yucky Moment: Frank gnaws off a tree branch with his teeth.

Frank's Room: ☺ 😐 ☹
Doug's Room: ☺ 😐 ☹

Miami: 168th/83rd Streets

Cast: Alex, Laurie, Dez, Ty

The Rooms: Laurie warms up a living room by painting the walls brick red with black and cream accents, building two large bookcases, hanging botanical prints, slipcovering the existing furniture, and using a faux-tortoiseshell finish on a coffee table. Dez adds drama to a bedroom by applying a "pan-Asian ethnic theme" featuring upholstered cornice boards, mosquito netting, and stenciled dragon lampshades.

Musical Moments: Laurie plays "Chopsticks" on the

homeowners' piano.

Conflict: Laurie's homeowners want to install a faux fireplace, and she vetoes it. The homeowners convince Ty to help them build a square frame and paint logs and a fire on it. They keep putting it in the room, and Laurie keeps removing it.

Notable: Dez falls ill with the flu on Day 2 and spends a lot of time sleeping on a couch. As a result, her team falls behind. Ty jumps in to help finish the room on time.

Oink?: Dez adds a large pink piggy bank that she dressed in a skirt and a wig.

Fashion Report: Dez wears an amazing large-brimmed hat during Designer Chat. It features black and white spots, fuzzy black trim, and a very tall white feather. She's outdone herself.

Laurie's Room: ☺ 😐 ☹
Dez's Room: ☺ 😐 ☹

Fort Lauderdale: 59th Street

Cast: Alex, Frank, Hildi, Ty

The Rooms: Frank adds "comfortable drama" to a living room, with bright orange textured walls, a mosaic-top coffee table, slipcovered furniture, and a large custom art project. Hildi goes retro in a Fiestaware collector's kitchen by building an acrylic table, adding period chairs, and hanging large globe light fixtures. She also installs a shelving unit to display the homeowner's collection.

Quotable Quote: Frank describes his coffee table design to Ty by saying, "If you were in Pompeii just before Vesuvius erupted and you grabbed a piece of furniture, it would be this table."

Design Insight: During Designer Chat, Alex points out that one of the legs on Frank's coffee table is a slightly different style than the other three. Frank claims that he designs all his furniture that way.

Notable: Hildi removes her first ceiling fan.

Fashion Report: Hildi wears a bikini top during the opening segment.

Frank's Room: ☺ 😐 ☹
Hildi's Room: ☺ 😐 ☹

Key West: Elizabeth Street

Cast: Alex, Frank, Genevieve, Ty

The Rooms: Frank adds a Caribbean touch to a living room by painting the walls light blue, adding a hand-painted mermaid, building a telephone table, and laying vinyl tiles. Gen makes a tiny living room appear larger with her "Caribbean Chill" design, which includes magenta walls with lime green accents, a large custom-built sectional sofa, and a wall decoupaged with pages torn from a 100-year-old book.

Conflict: Frank's homeowners take the reins and wind up running the show. (They also bring a blender with them, because they never travel without it.) They don't finish their homework, claiming a neighbor came over with champagne.

Quotable Quote: Frank describes the shifting control of the project as "Bad reception—it goes in and out."

Frank's Room: ☺ 😐 ☹
Gen's Room: ☺ 😐 ☹

Austin: Wycliff

Cast: Alex, Doug, Hildi, Amy Wynn

The Rooms: Doug creates a funky kitchen by painting the cabinets with blue and purple swirls, extending the existing countertop, applying blue and purple vinyl squares on the wall, and hanging numerous clocks (he titles the room "Time Flies"). Hildi adds drama to a dining room by covering the walls with brown felt, papering the ceiling with small, individual red and gold squares, covering the back of an armoire with dried bamboo leaves, and making custom light fixtures.

Tiff Time: At the start of the show, Doug hasn't created any drawings or taken any measurements and expects Amy

Wynn to cut all new cabinet doors by removing the old doors and tracing around them as templates. Amy Wynn complains to Alex that Doug thinks a carpenter is merely an assistant to a designer. Later, Amy Wynn makes a point of thanking Hildi for her detailed drawings.

Time Flies: Doug covers a wall with clocks set for different time zones around the world. When the homeowner asks where the clock batteries are, Doug realizes that he forgot to buy them and that he doesn't have money left to get any. He decides to set and hang the clocks, even though they aren't running.

Oops!: In order to paper the ceiling, one of Hildi's homeowners uses a pneumatic glue sprayer and accidentally glues his mask to his beard.

Doug's Room: ☺ ☺ ☹
Hildi's Room: ☺ ☺ ☹

Austin: Wing Road

Cast: Alex, Genevieve, Hildi, Amy Wynn

The Rooms: Gen goes south of the border in a kitchen by adding a mosaic tile backsplash, covering the cabinet door insets with textured tin, painting the floors terra-cotta, and painting the walls yellow. Hildi brightens a living room by applying a textured glaze over the existing gold paint, covering a wall in wooden squares, sewing silver slipcovers, and adding a cowhide rug.

The Power of Pots: Gen adds metallic touches by using colanders as light fixtures and covering a bar stool with a tall pasta pot.

Notable: Gen removes her first ceiling fan. Hildi removes her ceiling fan too.

Love Notes: Gen's male homeowner has a crush on Amy Wynn. Gen and the homeowner's wife tease him repeatedly in front of Amy Wynn.

Fashion Report: Amy Wynn wears two braids à la Laura Ingalls Wilder.

Gen's Room: ☺ ☺ ☹
Hildi's Room: ☺ ☺ ☹

Austin: Birdhouse Drive 🔌

Cast: Alex, Frank, Laurie, Amy Wynn

The Rooms: Frank enlivens a living room by painting three walls sage green, painting the fireplace wall shocking pink, installing floor-to-ceiling shelving on either side of the fireplace, adding a hand-painted checkerboard table, and making unique art pieces. Laurie divides a living/dining room with a suspended piece of fabric, paints the rooms with warm oranges and yellows, adds olive green accents, builds a bench seat, and creates a custom coffee table.

Girl Power: Amy Wynn introduces a female homeowner to a jigsaw.

Quotable Quote: Frank describes a wooden rooster he wants to make as "kind of a Frenchy, Mediterranean slash funk Texas rooster."

Time Crunch: During Designer Chat, Laurie confesses that she was running short on time and that the paint on the bench she and Alex are sitting on is still tacky. Laurie freaks a bit because she thinks she's sticking.

Notable: Day 1 is the anniversary of Frank's homeowners. The husband has flowers delivered to his wife, and Frank stays to do their homework that night so the homeowners can go out and celebrate. Oh, and Amy Wynn plays the saw.

Frank's Room: ☺ ☺ ☹
Laurie's Room: ☺ ☺ ☹

Orlando: Lake Catherine

Cast: Alex, Vern, Hildi, Ty

The Rooms: New guy Vern brings warmth and depth into a wine importer's kitchen by painting the walls with two shades of red, installing a custom-built wine rack, building a new chandelier using 36 wineglasses, and creating a new

tabletop. Hildi creates a sleek bedroom with gray walls, an aluminum foil ceiling, gray flannel curtains, bamboo curtain rods, and a black armoire covered in bamboo.

Oops!: One of Vern's homeowners juggles lemons and then breaks the vase he's putting them into.

Quotable Quote: When Ty teases Hildi about using too much hair spray, she responds, "Look who's talking, porcupine!"

Tweet Dreams: Hildi includes a live canary in her design and names the bird "Hildi."

Helpful Ty: One set of homeowners home-brew beer, and Ty keeps trying to tap their kegs.

Notable: In Vern's premiere episode, viewers are introduced to his perfectionist side: 1) He gives Ty several architectural drawings for what he wants created in the room. 2) After five coats of paint, he and his homeowners are still painting late on Day 2.

Vern's Room: ☺ ☺ ☹
Hildi's Room: ☺ ☺ ☹

Orlando: Gotha Furlong

Cast: Alex, Genevieve, Frank, Ty

The Rooms: Gen creates romance in a bedroom by adding a ceiling-height cedar plank headboard, butter yellow paint, throw pillows made from a 1970s tablecloth, and cedar bookshelves. Frank makes a bedroom feel "earthy, arty, and wonderful" by painting the walls tan, adding gauzy white fabric to the four-poster bed, building a cedar window seat with storage drawers, painting a floorcloth, and hand painting batik-print pillows.

Coincidence?: Gen and one of her homeowners attended the same art school but at different times.

Oops!: Gen tries to modify a ceiling fan by removing the existing blades and replacing them with woven fans. That doesn't work, so she uses silver rub on the blades and rehangs them.

Quotable Quote: Frank says, "You'd better get some popcorn and a good attitude, because this is something you wanna write home to your mother about."

Fashion Report: Ty has an especially bad hair day. Frank paints Alex's nails and says that he does the same for his wife all the time.

Notable: Gen's yellow paint gets on Alex's white pants. Explaining the entire process as she does it, Alex then covers up the spot with gaffer's tape so the other homeowners won't know what's happening in their home when she goes to help Frank.

Gen's Room: ☺ ☺ ☹
Frank's Room: ☺ ☺ ☹

Orlando: Winterhaven

Cast: Alex, Doug, Laurie, Ty

The Rooms: Laurie perks up a seldom used living room with yellow paint, sheer window treatments, a geometric wall design, and a large ottoman. Doug regresses to his childhood while decorating a boy's bedroom. Doug's design, "Americana Medley," includes red walls, a blue ceiling, stenciled stars and cow prints, a tree limb headboard, and a barn door window treatment.

Mean Streak?: One of Laurie's homeowners is afraid of heights, and Laurie keeps putting him on ladders.

Fashion Report: Doug wears a red scouting vest during Day 1; Ty dons a cowboy hat.

Sing Out!: One of Doug's homeowners turns 40. The cast brings him a cake and sings "Happy Birthday." Doug takes the harmony.

Diva Fit: Doug pouts on the couch because he didn't have his own bedroom growing up.

Quotable Quote: Ty tells Alex that Doug's full name is Douglas "Issues" Wilson.

Notable: AlexCam in hand, Alex stalks the boy whose bedroom Doug is designing. The boy hops on his bike and pedals away yelling, "Stay away from me!"

Doug's Room: ☺ ☺ ☹
Laurie's Room: ☺ ☺ ☹

Albuquerque: Gloria

Cast: Alex, Hildi, Doug, Ty

The Rooms: Hildi warms up a living room by painting the walls brown and copper, applying yellow fabric paint to the existing furniture, making a curtain rod from copper pipe, and installing an entertainment center. Doug sets sail in a living room ("Wind in Our Sails") by painting the walls slate gray, hanging white curtains, installing a banquette, and suspending a large white canvas from the ceiling.

Notable: Alex sings and plays guitar (badly!) for Doug. Doug responds by singing her a song: "Alex is gonna go places we don't want to go. She's gonna be lonely there, singing her sad, sad songs."

Fashion Report: The female homeowners sport blue and green nail polish and nail art that spells out "Trading Spaces."

Hildi's Room: ☺ ☺ ☹
Doug's Room: ☺ ☺ ☹

Santa Fe: Felize

Cast: Alex, Genevieve, Vern, Ty

The Rooms: Gen designs a modern Southwestern living room ("Adobe Mod") by adding white paint, a custom-built sofa, woven-rope end tables, and clay jars. Vern creates a calming oasis in a kitchen by painting the walls pale blue, installing a planter of wheat grass, laying parquet floor, hanging mirrors, and applying a stained-glass look to the cabinet doors.

Notable: Gen, Vern, and Ty ride horses during their introduction. Gen's homeowners smudge the room with sage after clearing the furniture from the room.

Hand-y Solution: Vern, his homeowners, and Alex rip up three layers of linoleum flooring to lay the parquet floor. Alex speeds up the process by prying up large portions of the floor with a hand truck.

Yuck!: Vern tastes the wheat grass, hates it, and tries to spit it out. Alex makes a wheat grass smoothie and hates it too.

Gen's Room: ☺ ☺ ☹
Vern's Room: ☺ ☺ ☹

New Orleans: Jacob Street

Cast: Alex, Laurie, Hildi, Amy Wynn

The Rooms: Laurie creates continuity and flow in a kitchen/office/dining/living room, using pale yellow paint on the walls, a 20-foot-long sisal rug, slipcovers, new kitchen storage, and a new furniture arrangement. Hildi modernizes a kitchen by painting the walls pistachio green, laying black vinyl tile, building a new island, and finding new uses for plumbing conduit.

Witchy-Poo: In the spirit of New Orleans, Alex cuts locks of hair from Hildi and Laurie to make voodoo dolls. Hildi is nonchalant about the hair loss. Laurie is shocked and looks like she's about to cry. After making the dolls, Alex sticks each doll in the butt to make the designers hurry up.

Notable: The owners of the multipurpose great-room—both the husband and the wife—cry.

Laurie's Room: ☺ ☺ ☹
Hildi's Room: ☺ ☺ ☹

New Orleans: Walter Road

Cast: Alex, Genevieve, Frank, Amy Wynn

The Rooms: Gen creates an antique look in a bedroom she titles "Bombay Meets Étouffée." She paints the walls peach and pea green, installs a vintage beaded chandelier, and applies an antique gold finish to cornice boards and bookshelves. Frank updates a kitchen by removing garish wallpaper, coating the walls with textured tan paint, painting cabinet drawers in red and green, coiling copper wire around the existing drawer pulls, and installing a large family bulletin board.

Fashion Report: Gen reveals her numerous fabrics to the homeowners by walking into the room wearing the different cloths around her head, waist, and arms.

Oops!: Frank gets stuck in the pantry while he and his team move the refrigerator; he has to shimmy out a small window.

Huh?: Frank titles his room "Beaver Cleaver Meets George Jetson," but there's no apparent reason why. Also, Frank repeatedly uses a paper bag as a puppet.

Measuring Up: Frank measures a space in a room by lying on the floor and stretching his arms over his head. He tells Amy Wynn the length is "one fat man with arms extended."

Girl Power: Amy Wynn tries to teach a fearful female homeowner how to use a screw gun.

Quotable Quotes: It's a tie between Frank and, well, Frank. On the challenge of finishing on budget: "I feel like someone's given me a wad of chewing gum and said, 'Go fill up the Grand Canyon'"; on the public's perception of designers: "If somebody tells me that a designer is just this little guy who goes around fluffing flowers, I intend to break every bone in his body and make a lamp out of him."

Gen's Room: ☺ 😐 ☹
Frank's Room: ☺ 😐 ☹

New Orleans: D'evereaux Street

Cast: Alex, Vern, Genevieve, Amy Wynn

The Rooms: Vern kicks up the style in a boys' bedroom with a black and white soccer theme. He paints the walls black and white, upholsters the headboards, creates two desk stations, suspends soccer balls from the ceiling, and lays a black and white vinyl floor complete with a custom soccer ball medallion. Gen heads back to the 1960s in her "Retro Fly" den/guest room by painting multicolor stripes on the walls, hanging retro light fixtures, slipcovering an existing futon, and separating the desk area from the seating area with a chain-link screen.

Quotable Quote: Vern consults with the younger boy at the start of the show. Scotty tells Vern he wants to become an architect. Vern gives him a high five and tells him that "[Architects] get all the women."

Oops!: When Vern believes he has received one twin- and one full-size bed frame, he calls the store and claims he received the wrong thing. Alex mentions in the voice-over that Vern later discovers the full frame is adjustable.

Oops! Part 2: Amy Wynn waits until the end of Day 2 to finish a set of bookshelves, forgetting that Gen needs time to paint them. The shelves are hanging at the end of the show, but there's nothing on them because they're still wet.

Mean Streak?: Alex plays soccer with the two little boys and tells them that the girls in their classes at school will love the new bedroom because it's a "girlie room." The boys knock her to the ground.

Notable: Gen and her homeowners have problems finding wall studs. When their electronic stud finder stops working, they start drilling random holes to find the studs.

Vern's Room: ☺ 😐 ☹
Gen's Room: ☺ 😐 ☹

New York: Shore Road 😖 ♥

Cast: Alex, Genevieve, Dez, Amy Wynn

The Rooms: Gen looks to the East for inspiration on a sun porch and creates a tearoom atmosphere with a new sake bar, a seating area, and several organic accents. Dez gives a living room her version of "country with a French twist" by painting the walls yellow, stenciling fern leaves around the room, slipcovering the existing sofa, adding a planter of grass, and hanging geometric window treatments.

Good-Bye: This is Dez's final appearance on *Trading Spaces*.

Silly Gen!: Gen tries to use pieces of bamboo as accents, but they keep falling apart on her. She gets a serious case of the

 giggles. Gen later tries to cut down a stalk of bamboo from the homeowners' yard with what looks like a serrated steak knife.

Oops!: Attempting to shine the sunporch floor, Alex loses control of an electric floor buffer, screams, and eventually falls to the ground.

Oops! Part 2: As Alex huddles near an outdoor fire to get warm, smoke starts to drift toward her, and something gets in her eye. She turns away and complains of being blinded. Amy Wynn later roasts marshmallows on the fire.

Notable: The sunporch homeowners like their room so much, they dance The Monkey.

Gen's Room: ☺ 😐 ☹
Dez's Room: ☺ 😐 ☹

New York: Sherwood Drive  ♥

Cast: Alex, Vern, Doug, Amy Wynn

The Rooms: Vern creates a serene bedroom by painting the walls lilac-blue, making a television cabinet out of picture frames, hanging yards of indigo velvet, installing sconces containing live Beta fish above the bed, and creating a 4-foot wall clock out of candle sconces and battery-operated clock hands. Doug designs a relaxing "Zen-sational" bedroom by hanging grass cloth on the walls, making light fixtures out of Malaysian baskets, hanging a full-length mirror on an angle, and building a 6-foot fountain.

Fan Notes: Vern removes his first ceiling fan and replaces it with a five-armed beaded chandelier.

Notable: Homeowner dissension abounds in this episode! Doug's mother-daughter homeowners tell him that they both have dates and need to stop working at 5 p.m. Doug and Alex explain that the homeowners agreed to complete all the work necessary to redo the room when they signed up for the show. The next morning, the homeowners complain to Doug about the hard work they had to do the night before. However, they don't know that Doug stopped by the previous night and found that they had recruited friends to do their homework for them. After a scolding from Doug, the daughter homeowner lashes back, saying "When I get married, I will never pull up carpet, ever!" Doug leaves in a huff while the homeowners make faces at him.

Vern's Room: ☺ 😐 ☹
Doug's Room: ☺ 😐 ☹

New York: Linda Court

Cast: Alex, Doug, Frank, Amy Wynn

The Rooms: Doug creates a Mediterranean-flavored living room by covering the walls in yellow Venetian plaster, making custom lamps, building a large armoire to match an existing one, and weaving strips of wood through metal conduit for a woven-wall effect. Frank also heads to the Mediterranean in a living room, applying a faux finish with three shades of yellow paint, then adding stenciled squares on the walls, a faux fresco created from drywall, and gondola-inspired lamps.

Resourceful: Doug's and Frank's designs are so close in concept that Doug sends Alex over to Frank's to borrow some teal and black paint.

Quotable Quote: Alex nags Frank, saying "Time is money!" He responds, "Let me write that down so I can embroider that on a whoopee cushion."

Doug's Room: ☺ 😐 ☹
Frank's Room: ☺ 😐 ☹

New Jersey: Sam Street

Cast: Alex, Laurie, Hildi, Ty

The Rooms: Laurie warms up a dining room with yellow paint, shades of berries and pinks as accents, a custom-built cornice board, and cream paint on the existing furniture. Hildi adds drama and romance to a bedroom by painting the walls a yellowed sage green, bringing in several sage silk fabrics, adding a sofa upholstered in burgundy fabric, extending the existing headboard, and building "pillow pod" seating.

Lucky Laurie: Laurie removes the existing upholstery from

---

the dining room chairs and finds a pretty yellow fabric that matches her design perfectly.

Budget Booster: Hildi reupholsters a couch she brought with her from Georgia. She keeps pulling coins from the cushions and adding them to her budget.

Hildi's Design Theory: "I usually try to find the biggest or the boldest thing that is going to make the most dramatic change."

Notable: Ty and Alex spend most of the episode running through the woods looking for the legendary Jersey Devil. Laurie does a very bad approximation of a Jersey accent.

Laurie's Room: ☺ 😐 ☹
Hildi's Room: ☺ 😐 ☹

New Jersey: Lincroft 😖

Cast: Alex, Laurie, Doug, Ty

The Rooms: Laurie adds style and function to a small kitchen by laying parquet vinyl flooring, painting the walls an ocher yellow, wall-mounting the microwave oven, painting the cabinets white, and creating a home office/family message center. Doug softens a very red living room by painting the walls sandy taupe, adding wooden strips to accentuate the ceiling height, painting colorful checkerboard designs on coffee tables, sewing several brightly colored rag rugs together to create a large carpet, and designing a wooden candleholder using a rope-and-pulley system. He titles the look "Country Kaleidoscope."

Oops!: Laurie attempts to remove yet another ceiling fan, but it falls to the floor and breaks.

¿Cómo?: Laurie and Ty try to put together a lighting fixture using directions written in Spanish.

Quotable Quote: When Doug's homeowners express concern about the many different accent colors he's using, he responds by saying, "It's not as obnoxious as it could be."

Notable: Alex decides that Doug isn't working fast enough, so she takes over his lamp project. She starts talking to the camera about the project but can't get her pliers open. Doug (in the background) starts doing Alex's job, introducing the episode. He mispronounces things. They decide to keep their regular jobs.

Laurie's Room: ☺ 😐 ☹
Doug's Room: ☺ 😐 ☹

New Jersey: Lafayette Street

Cast: Alex, Frank, Vern, Ty

The Rooms: Frank adds Victorian elements to a dining/living room by painting the walls pink with burgundy accents, showcasing the homeowners' collection of wooden houses, applying decorative molding to the existing entertainment center, and creating original wall art using basic woodcarving skills. Vern softens in a living room, making it baby-friendly. He paints the walls two shades of sage green, builds a large ottoman that doubles as a coffee table, builds a sofa out of a mattress, suspends a mantel for the fireplace, and adds bright blue accents.

Good-Bye: This is Alex's last appearance on *Trading Spaces*.

Notable: Frank is absolutely unquotable in this episode.

Huh?: Vern blows up pictures of the homeowners' baby and uses them as lampshades on three wall lamps.

Swede Thing: Vern attempts to put together an armoire, but the instructions are in Swedish. He convinces Ty to put it together, pointing out that Ty looks more like the man in the illustrations.

Bet Me!: Ty and Alex wager a massage on which designer will finish first. Alex takes Vern, and Ty takes Frank. Both Alex and Ty are underhanded in trying to influence the contest. Ty wins.

Frank's Room: ☺ 😐 ☹
Vern's Room: ☺ 😐 ☹

Season 2

Quakertown: Quaker's Way

Cast: Paige, Doug, Hildi, Ty

The Rooms: Doug goes "ball-istic" in a living room, painting the walls lime green, building a custom sofa complete with bowling ball feet, hanging a wall of mirrors, making custom lamps out of gazing balls, and adding brown and blue accents. Hildi introduces viewers to the concept of orthogonal design by painting perpendicular lines on the walls and ceiling of a basement, creating a nine-piece sectional seating area, and screening off a large storage area.

Notable: The Season 2 premiere introduces the graphic opening credits, the outtakes during the end credits, and the *Trading Spaces*/TLC/Banyan Productions trailer outside the carpentry area.

Fashion Report: Ty sports a mustache.

Having a Ball: Doug quickly becomes frustrated while trying to create a decorative piece by wrapping wire around a kick ball. Giving up, he kicks the ball (and the wire) over the fence into a neighbor's yard.

Having a Ball, Part 2: Doug and Ty set a good example by stealing a gazing ball (for Doug's lamp project) from a neighbor's yard. Ty distracts the neighbor, and Doug runs up and steals the gazing ball. Doug tells Paige during Designer Chat that he returned the stolen ball and purchased similar balls to complete his project.

Huh?: Hildi carts her lumber from the carpentry area to her room in a little red wagon.

What Was She Thinking?: Although she knows the homeowners have small children, Hildi makes wall art out of acrylic box frames filled with different types of candy.

Tuneful: Doug plays the sax, Hildi plays the drums, and Ty plays guitar during the opening segment.

Doug's Room: 😊 😐 ☹
Hildi's Room: 😊 😐 ☹

New Jersey: Tall Pines Drive 💣 🙁 🔌

Cast: Paige, Laurie, Vern, Amy Wynn

The Rooms: Laurie experiments with several paint colors in a basement by painting a Matisse-inspired mural. She also makes a chalkboard-top kids' table, installs an art station, creates curtains out of place mats, and hangs louvered panels as a room screen. Vern designs a love nest in a bedroom by hanging brown upholstered wall squares, sewing lush draperies, painting the existing furniture white, installing silver candle chandeliers, and adding new bedside tables.

Time Crunch: Laurie stresses often about the mural and at one point says, "Can I just, like, blink and click my heels and this'll be done?"

Yucky Moment: Vern's homeowner loves his design choices so much that she moans as he shows her paint and fabric options.

Notable: A human-size nutcracker named Nutty resides in Laurie's room. Nutty stays in the room during the first half of Day I, and because one homeowner feels that Nutty is staring at him, he paints over one of Nutty's eyes. Later, Nutty floats on a raft in a swimming pool. He makes a final appearance in the passenger seat of a golf cart driven by Amy Wynn.

Laurie's Room: 😊 😐 ☹
Vern's Room: 😊 😐 ☹

Maple Glen: Fiedler Road

Cast: Paige, Laurie, Genevieve, Amy Wynn

The Rooms: Laurie paints the walls of a bedroom celadon green, creates a headboard from white and yellow silk squares, paints the existing furniture white, installs bamboo pieces as door hardware, and converts bamboo place mats into pillow shams. Using lilies as inspiration in a living room, Gen paints the

---

walls a yellowed taupe, builds two new couches and a new coffee table, hangs large black and white family photos, and pins prints of vintage botanical postcards to the wall.

Fan-natic: Laurie removes the ceiling fan, and her homeowners protest loudly.

Attitude Check: Laurie repeatedly says she's "in a panic mode" about her room; Gen says she's in a "slo-mo hot zone," meaning that the high room temperature is making her zone out.

Laurie's Room: 😊 😐 ☹
Gen's Room: 😊 😐 ☹

Northampton: James Avenue

Cast: Paige, Hildi, Frank, Ty

The Rooms: Hildi updates a living room with mustard-gold paint, aubergine curtains, yellow and red tufted pillows, a sisal rug, sunflowers, and a river rock mosaic fireplace. Frank creates a nautical Nantucket theme in a living room by painting the walls pale sage, adding yellow and seafoam green pillows, wrapping rope around the coffee table legs to make the table resemble a pier, and building a dinghy-inspired dog bed.

Oops!: Hildi tries to use an industrial sander/scraper, but it won't turn to the right. Pandemonium breaks out as Hildi, Ty, and the male homeowner attempt to get the scraper to work correctly. Eventually, Ty runs it in left-hand circles while Hildi and the homeowner run around holding the cord to keep it from wrapping around Ty.

Amen: Frank and his homeowners say a prayer to the paint gods, thanking them for their color choice.

Quotable Quote: Frank: "OK, I'll work this in between my tennis match with the royal family and my tanning appointment."

Tool Time: Frank encourages his male homeowner to keep sewing, telling him to think of the machine as another power tool. The homeowner decides to think of it as a jigsaw.

Yucky Moment: Both sets of homeowners like their rooms, but the homeowners who get the dark yellow living room are concerned that the paint color looks like a dirty diaper.

Hildi's Room: 😊 😐 ☹
Frank's Room: 😊 😐 ☹

Providence: Phillips Street

Cast: Paige, Hildi, Vern, Amy Wynn

The Rooms: Hildi adds sophistication to a living room by painting the walls slate gray, making butter yellow slipcovers, adding a touch of charcoal wax to an existing coffee table and side tables, and replacing the drop ceiling tiles with wood-tone panels. Vern uses the principles of feng shui in a living room by painting the walls and ceiling yellow for wealth, designing a coffee table that holds bamboo stalks for health, attaching small framed mirrors to the ceiling above a candle chandelier, and building a custom fish tank stand for the homeowner's large aquarium.

Girl Fight: Tensions mount between Hildi and Amy Wynn, who disagree on the best way to measure and cut ceiling tiles. Both have good points, but neither hears the other's opinions.

Lucky Vern: Vern removes the existing slipcover on the couch and discovers that the original upholstery color is cranberry, which perfectly matches his design.

Navel Alert!: Paige exposes her belly button while attaching Vern's mirrors to the ceiling.

Notable: Paige is nearly attacked by bees during the key swap.

Hildi's Room: 😊 😐 ☹
Vern's Room: 😊 😐 ☹

Providence: Wallis Avenue 💣 😈 🔌

Cast: Paige, Genevieve, Frank, Amy Wynn

The Rooms: Gen brings a touch of Tuscany to a bedroom by painting the walls sage green, painting the ceiling yellow, installing floor-to-ceiling shelves, hanging ivy above the headboard, and using light and airy curtains and bed linens.

Frank enlivens a kitchen by using several pastel shades of paint, creating a larger tabletop, laying a vinyl floor, and adding painted chevrons to the cabinets.

Hard Work: Frank sweats so much during Day I that he says, "I had a kid walk by and throw a coin in my mouth and make a wish."

Notable: Frank uses his budget sparingly in order to buy the homeowners a dishwasher (they don't have one, and they have two kids). When Amy Wynn tells him that she can return two pieces of wood and enable him to buy the appliance, he does a touchdown victory dance. To save installation time, the dishwasher is wheeled in with a bow on the box during The Reveal.

Quotable Quote: Frank predicts the homeowners' reaction to the new dishwasher: "The squealing is gonna be like the Chicago stockyards when they see this."

Gen's Room: 😊 😐 ☹
Frank's Room: 😊 😐 ☹

Boston: Ashfield Street ♥

Cast: Paige, Laurie, Genevieve, Ty

The Rooms: Laurie breathes new life into a kids' room by painting the walls lavender, creating a trundle bed, painting the existing furniture white, and using ribbons as accents. Gen adds a Moroccan touch to a kid's room by painting the walls and ceiling deep blue, installing a large curtained bed, hanging a Moroccan metal lamp, using gold fabric accents, and hanging white draperies.

Shocker!: Laurie thinks she has a serious problem when she discovers the wood floors are a pale yellow and not the warm honey color she believed them to be.

Oops!: Paige drills through a plastic place mat to create a lampshade, but the bit comes out of the drill. When Gen tries to pull the bit out of the place mat, she finds that they've drilled through the homeowners' deck. A huge giggle fit ensues.

Notable: Gen returns the morning of Day 2 to find that her homeowner (who is an electrician) has installed two electrical outlets in the freshly painted room. The paint job is messed up, and the homeowner has left insulation and plaster shards all over the floor.

Happy Ending: The girls who live in Laurie's room like her design so much that they actually turn cartwheels.

Laurie's Room: 😊 😐 ☹
Gen's Room: 😊 😐 ☹

Springfield: Sunset Terrace 💣

Cast: Paige, Hildi, Vern, Ty

The Rooms: Hildi creates a Victorian look in a living room by painting the walls light putty, using blue and white print fabric for draperies and slipcovers, painting blue stripes on the wood floor, sewing a white faux-fur rug, and transforming the fireplace with a custom-built Victorian-style mantelpiece. Vern goes for an even more Victorian look in the other living room by painting the walls yellow, highlighting the homeowners' French provincial furniture, laying a Victorian rug, making a light fixture with silver mesh and hand-strung beads, and creating a custom art piece using celestial and fleur-de-lis stencils.

Navel Alert!: Paige shoots a basketball during the introduction and exposes her belly button.

Notable: Hildi and Vern design against type in this episode, with mixed results.

Hildi's Room: 😊 😐 ☹
Vern's Room: 😊 😐 ☹

Boston: Institute Road

Cast: Paige, Doug, Frank, Ty

The Rooms: Doug looks to the leaves for inspiration in his "Autumnal Bliss" bedroom. He papers the walls with bark paper, upholsters the headboard in linen, hangs yellow linen draperies, and frames fall leaves as art. Frank creates a Shakespearean library by painting the walls red, hand-painting Elizabethan musician cutouts for the walls, and painting a rounded stone pattern on the floor.

Traveling Companions: Doug goes to find autumn leaves with Paige and Ty. Doug drives the golf cart, Paige sits on the back, and Ty rides on a skateboard by holding on to a string tied to the back of the cart.

Not Listening: Doug tries to explain his leaf art project to Paige, who keeps jumping on a trampoline in the background and saying, "Yeah, yeah, yeah."

Quotable Quotes: Frank, on what may be under the carpet he's ripping up: "It could be the gates of heaven or the portals of hell." Frank again, on his love of red paint: "Throw me on the ground and make me write a bad check."

Wise Words: One of Frank's homeowners picks out a Shakespearean quote to paint above the bookshelves: "All things are ready if our minds be so."

Notable: Ty skeletons down the driveway on a wheeled ottoman multiple times, nearly crashing into piles of lumber.

Doug's Room: ☺ ☺ ☹
Frank's Room: ☺ ☺ ☹

Philadelphia: Jeannes Street

Cast: Paige, Genevieve, Vern, Amy Wynn

The Rooms: Gen turns a basement den into a 3-D *Scrabble* board by painting taupe and white grids on the floors and ceiling, installing a black wall-length bar, making pillows that mimic *Scrabble* board squares, and framing game boards to hang on the wall. Vern uses the holiday season for inspiration in a living room by painting the walls and ceiling deep red, making camel slipcovers and draperies, and building a dark wood armoire with mirrored doors.

Silly Gen!: Gen and Paige try to screw lazy Susan tops to bar stools. First, Gen's screws aren't long enough; then they can't get the screws in, and Gen realizes she has the drill in reverse; next their screws are too long, and the tops won't swivel. A huge giggle fit breaks out.

Conflict: Vern's female homeowner gives him grief about painting the ceiling. She also wants to build radiator covers. Vern draws up plans to do so, but Amy Wynn can't complete the work in time. The homeowner is very unhappy about it.

Time Test: Vern's male homeowner takes forever to wrap lights around two mini pine trees.

Gen's Room: ☺ ☺ ☹
Vern's Room: ☺ ☺ ☹

New Jersey: Perth Road

Cast: Paige, Frank, Laurie, Amy Wynn

The Rooms: Frank gives a living room a homier feel by adding light camel paint, a coffee table topped with a picture frame, textured folk art on the wall, and a custom-built armoire ("It's kind of a puppet theater cathedral"). Laurie redoes a bedroom without altering the existing Queen Anne furniture. She paints the walls a warm apricot, builds a custom canopy that rests on top of the four-poster bed, and adds bookshelves as nightstands.

Say What?: Frank describes his design as a "formal, casual, yet funky over-the-top look."

Girl Power: Frank's female homeowner learns to use a jigsaw.

Boys Club: Frank's male homeowner complains about having to sew, because he doesn't think it's a manly activity. However, he also points out that he's secure in his manhood. Frank retorts, "Well, then if you're so damned secure, start putting that stuffing in that pillow."

Quotable Quote: While cutting tree branches to use in his room, Frank says, "I have a college degree. Reduced to a beaver."

Fashion Report: Laurie straightens her hair for this episode.

Notable: Laurie's female homeowner is a former Philadelphia Eagles cheerleader.

Making Do: Laurie is "freaking out" because her swing-arm lamps haven't arrived by the morning of Day 2. She tells Paige that she has called to track the package but the tracking wasn't helpful. She then waits on the street looking for the delivery truck. The lamps never arrive, and she has to substitute discount store fixtures.

Frank's Room: ☺ ☺ ☹
Laurie's Room: ☺ ☺ ☹

Maryland: Village Green

Cast: Paige, Genevieve, Doug, Amy Wynn

The Rooms: Gen refines a bedroom by painting one wall chocolate brown, covering the ceiling with gold metallic paint, installing a custom geometric shelving unit, making a fountain, decoupaging sewing patterns to a wall, and creating a light fixture out of a large wicker ball. Doug creates an elegant and sophisticated look in a bedroom by painting the walls gray, building a large upholstered headboard with storage in the back, painting the furniture white, and painting large Matisse-inspired figures directly on the wall.

Oops!: To create custom lampshades, Gen wraps rounded glass vases with plastic wrap and then winds glued string around them à la papier-mâché. Once the vases are dry, Gen and Paige put on safety glasses and start hammering the shades to break the vases on the inside. Gen thinks her idea of including the plastic wrap will keep them from having to touch any shards of glass. She's wrong. After a huge giggle fit, Gen looks into the camera and warns, "This project isn't for kids."

Name Game: Doug titles his room "Strip Stripe" for the gray and white striped fabric he uses to cover the headboard.

Reveal-ing Moment: The gray bedroom homeowners love their room, but the brown bedroom homeowners don't like theirs. In fact, the female homeowner doesn't like anything but the fountain and says that the sewing patterns will go the next day.

Gen's Room: ☺ ☺ ☹
Doug's Room: ☺ ☺ ☹

Maryland: Fairway Court

Cast: Paige, Vern, Doug, Amy Wynn

The Rooms: Vern softens a bedroom by painting the walls a soft gray, hanging charcoal draperies, suspending a canopy over the existing sleigh bed, and dangling 100 clear crystals from the canopy edge. Doug designs a fantasy bedroom suite for train enthusiasts by rounding the ceiling edges, covering the walls with blue paint and fabric, and building fake walls and windows to mimic the inside of a Pullman car.

Navel Alert!: Paige exposes her belly button while reaching up to touch the hanging crystals.

Quotable Quote: Vern states during Designer Chat, "Precision doesn't have to go overtime; you just have to be well-planned."

Fashion Report: Doug's hair is super slicked back.

Notable: Doug claims that this design is the biggest challenge he's taken on in a *Trading Spaces* episode. Paige refers to it as a "marvelous achievement."

Vern's Room: ☺ ☺ ☹
Doug's Room: ☺ ☺ ☹

Chicago: Edward Road

Cast: Paige, Frank, Laurie, Ty

The Rooms: Frank adds patina to a kitchen by using touches of terra-cotta, copper, and green paint. He also lays earth-tone vinyl flooring, paints a faux-tile backsplash, makes a large floorcloth, and makes a butcher-block island. Laurie gives a living room a touch of European flair by painting a faux-fresco finish in yellow tones, installing dark wooden beams on the ceiling, hanging burlap draperies, painting a faux-inlay top on an occasional table, and

repeating an X motif throughout the room.

Quotable Quote: At the end of Day 1 Frank says, "I'm gonna go home, have a pedicure, manicure, shower, have my designer stylist come in and...I'll see you in the morning."

Navel Alert!: Paige exposes her navel while salsa dancing with Frank's male homeowner.

Laurie's Design Theory: "I want to give them a room that is a basic skeleton with beautiful walls, the layout the way I think it needs to be...and then, hopefully, what I trigger them to do...[is get] a new love seat."

Frank's Room: ☺ ☺ ☹
Laurie's Room: ☺ ☺ ☹

Chicago: Spaulding Avenue 😈

Cast: Paige, Doug, Hildi, Ty

The Rooms: Doug adds a little funk to a living room by painting the walls yellow, using Venetian plaster to make black and yellow blocks on a wall, upholstering the furniture with zebra-print fabric, and suspending a tabletop from the ceiling to create a dining area. Hildi brings the outdoors into a bedroom. She paints the walls cream and the trim a deep plum and then draws large "swooshes" of grass on the walls with pastels. She adds a row of grass planter boxes along one wall, uses bursts of orange in pillows, and installs a large wooden bed.

Quick Shot: During the introductory segment, in a very brief shot, Hildi and Ty hit Doug in the face with a dart.

Bold Idea: Doug announces he's going to take a "risk" by hanging a large framed mirror above the fireplace.

Conflict: Doug wants to glaze a 2-inch border around the wood floor. He paints a small strip to show what it will look like, and the homeowners argue against it. He wipes it off with a pouty face.

Sticky Situation: After drawing grass blades on the wall, Hildi and her homeowners seal the chalk pastel with several cans of hair spray.

Oops!: Ty can't get the window bench into the bedroom. He eventually has to remove the center legs to get it inside the bedroom door.

Doug's Room: ☺ ☺ ☹
Hildi's Room: ☺ ☺ ☹

Chicago: Fairview Avenue

Cast: Paige, Vern, Genevieve, Ty

The Rooms: Vern brightens a kitchen by painting the walls pear green, painting the cabinets white, creating a new cabinet for storage, making a new table, laying a black and white geometric rug, upholstering a storage bench that doubles as seating at the table, and hanging upholstered cushions against the wall above the bench. Gen gives the lodge look to a basement living room by painting the walls cinnamon, installing a pine plank ceiling, hanging wood wainscoting, slipcovering the furniture, and highlighting the fireplace with built-in shelves.

Navel Alert!: Paige exposes her navel when she reaches up to help with Gen's ceiling.

Silly Gen!: Gen tries to dye white fabric orange to use as slipcovers. She and her female homeowner spend a great deal of time working on it, and it comes out pink.

Oops!: Gen breaks the heel of her boot and goes to Ty for the repair.

Rest Time: Ty tries to take a break on a school bus, and Gen has to drag him back to work.

Notable: Paige and Gen agree during Designer Chat that the living room Gen designed is closest to her own personal style.

Vern's Room: ☺ ☺ ☹
Gen's Room: ☺ ☺ ☹

Colorado: Berry Avenue

Cast: Paige, Genevieve, Hildi, Amy Wynn

The Rooms: Gen paints the walls of a kitchen bright eggplant, paints the cabinets vanilla-sage, removes the center panels of the cabinet doors to showcase the dishes inside, and prints each family member's face on a chair cover for personalized seating. Hildi creates an intimate living room by painting the walls a deep chocolate brown, using sage fabrics, transforming the coffee table into a large ottoman, and installing a wall-size fountain made to mimic the existing windows.

Yucky Moment: Gen explains her color choices by tearing apart a boiled artichoke. Paige later enters the room and mistakenly pops the bitter heart into her mouth. She quickly spits it out.

Resourceful: Gen sketches her table design—including measurements—on Amy Wynn's palm.

Great Taste: Hildi brushes melted chocolate on the wall as her homeowners enter at the beginning of the show. She then paints the wall with the chocolate brown paint that they'll be using.

Joke Time: Gen's homeowners rent a jackhammer and use it in a bucket of hardened concrete to make their neighbors think their floor is being ripped out.

Joke Time, Part 2: In an attempt to get back at Gen's team for using the jackhammer, Hildi's homeowners remove the music rack from the piano and have Paige take it to one of Gen's homeowners.

Technical Stuff: Gen attempts to explain how she uses her laptop to reproduce the family photos for the chair covers. Paige asks several questions, and Gen isn't really able to answer them. Gen describes the computer program she's using as a "special program for a special girl."

Silly Stuff: During Designer Chat, Paige and Gen wear the chair covers with the homeowners' faces over their heads and role-play the homeowners' reaction to their new room.

What Was She Thinking?: Hildi and Paige cover the bottom of a plastic window box planter with silicone to seal it. When they try to set a large piece of glass in the box to create the fountain, Paige cuts through the silicone, breaking the seal. Water quickly seeps across the wood floor. (After cleaning up the mess, Hildi decides to use two layers of pond lining to seal the planter.)

Gen's Room: 🙂 😐 🙁

Hildi's Room: 🙂 😐 🙁

Colorado: Cherry Street

Cast: Paige, Genevieve, Laurie, Amy Wynn

The Rooms: Gen gives a living room a punch of personality by painting the walls brick red with sage accents, hanging antlers on the walls, installing floor-to-ceiling shelving, making a focal point out of one of the homeowners' landscape photos, and creating an inlaid rug. Laurie applies a touch of mod to a living room by painting gray and yellow horizontal stripes on the walls, building a new glass-top coffee table, hanging silver silk draperies, and adding a piece of custom artwork.

Quotable Quote: Gen describes the original look of her room by saying, "If this were a country, it would be Beigeland."

What Was She Thinking?: Rather than lay a green rug on top of the beige carpet, Gen cuts out a patch of the carpet and lays the new rug inside. Gen warns viewers, "Don't do this if you're renting." Amy Wynn walks by while they're cutting the carpeting and says under her breath, "Wow. That's scary-looking."

Time Crunch: Laurie spends most of Day I laying out tape to form the horizontal paint lines. Laurie also has several plans to add storage to the room, but there is not enough time or wood to make her plans a reality.

My Way: Laurie, Paige, and Laurie's homeowners voice differing opinions on how to hang a large abstract canvas. Laurie finally tells them to hang it her way, because "I'm the designer."

Fashion Report: Laurie wears an extra-frilly pirate shirt during Designer Chat.

Gen's Room: 🙂 😐 🙁

Laurie's Room: 🙂 😐 🙁

Colorado: Andes Way

Cast: Paige, Frank, Vern, Amy Wynn

The Rooms: Frank creates a family-friendly living room by rag-rolling the walls with cream and peach paint, hanging valances coated with brown builder's paper, building a white and sage armoire, and creating a kids' nook with a large art table, plant murals on the walls, and wooden clouds nailed to the ceiling. Vern stripes a living room, laying two colors of laminate flooring in alternating stripes, painting a red horizontal stripe on the khaki walls, and continuing the same stripe across the draperies.

Say What?: Describing his paint technique, Frank says, "It's kinda, like, goth-eyed wonky."

Notable: Amy Wynn participates in Frank's crafts project, helping him cover the valance with builder's paper. She gives up after trying to adhere the paper without using crafts glue, and Frank calls her a "craft wimp."

Frank's Room: 🙂 😐 🙁

Vern's Room: 🙂 😐 🙁

Colorado: Stoneflower Drive

Cast: Paige, Frank, Doug, Amy Wynn

The Rooms: Frank injects some whimsy into a bedroom by painting the walls celadon green, building a large headboard that mimics a skyline, creating a matching dog bed, and hanging gold curtains. Doug updates a living room with a design he calls "Smoke Screen." He paints the walls moss green, removes colonial molding, adds pewter accents, hangs pleated metal screening, and builds screen doors to cover shelving around the fireplace.

Gotcha!: Frank brings in tacky dolphin pillows, and the homeowner says that she loves them. Frank laughs and explains that he's only using them as inexpensive pillow forms.

Dog Decor: Frank justifies his dog bed design by saying, "Try and get the feeling of what it would be like if you were a dog and you were lying in your bed going, 'I need a little wall decor here.'"

Helping Out: Doug lounges in a deck chair drinking iced tea while reading faux-finish directions to his homeowners. He tosses them supplies instead of getting up.

Wise Words: Frank, during Designer Chat: "I wanted to give them a room that has, like most relationships or marriages, some whimsy, some peacefulness, and a little bit of tactile sensitivity and sexuality."

Notable: Amy Wynn finishes all of her carpentry projects and decides to help Frank paint the dog bed. She admits to Paige that she's enjoying it.

Frank's Room: 🙂 😐 🙁

Doug's Room: 🙂 😐 🙁

Seattle: 137th Street

Cast: Paige, Doug, Frank, Ty

The Rooms: Doug does "Denim Deluxe" in a living room. He paints a white grid pattern on chocolate walls, slipcovers the furniture with brown and ivory denim, makes art pieces with brightly colored tissue paper, lowers the existing coffee table, installs white wainscoting, and builds a white facade to cover the brick fireplace. Frank brightens a living room by painting the walls reddish orange and yellow, installing a new mantel, hanging shelves on either side of the fireplace, making a fireplace screen painted with folk art characters, and creating a window valance with place mats and clothespins.

Quotable Quote: Frank greets his homeowners by saying, "What are we going to do to rip this room to shreds for two days and have a good time doing it?"

Conflict: Homeowner dissension abounds in this classic episode! The living room homeowners leave Doug strict instructions not to paint their fireplace, but of course, Doug wants to paint it white. His homeowners repeatedly argue with him about it. When Doug states that he's not happy, one of his homeowners turns ultrapositive and says, "It's OK not to be happy sometimes!" She suggests covering the fireplace with fabric, noting "You guys love cloth!" When Doug leaves the room in a huff, she looks to the camera and says, "Well, now he's a little cranky."

Resourceful?: While Doug pouts, Ty problem-solves by designing a facade to "slipcover" the brick. As he and Ty are installing the facade, Doug prophetically says, "This may be my shining moment."

Fashion Report: While working outside, Doug sports a denim jacket with the collar turned up.

Nasty Side: While working with Paige and his homeowners to make the tissue paper art, Doug places a wooden Santa figure on the table and says that he brought Frank along to oversee their crafting.

Huh?: Frank describes what he wants to paint on the walls by saying, "We're going to be doing a kind of rectangular, kind of checky, not really country, not really contemporary, just homey, cottagey, but with a kind of a more upbeat level."

Fashion Report: Heavy rain on Day 2 soaks Ty's pants up to midcalf.

Reveal-ing Moments: A classic Reveal that must be seen to be believed! The denim living room homeowners are extremely disappointed with their room (the male homeowner surmises Doug's design as "I see a lot of firewood"), and the female homeowner leaves the room in tears while her microphone continues running. The episode has a somewhat happy ending, with the male homeowner noting that "at least the room isn't orthogonal [like one of Hildi's infamous designs]."

Doug's Room: 🙂 😐 🙁

Frank's Room: 🙂 😐 🙁

Seattle: Dakota Street

Cast: Paige, Vern, Laurie, Ty

The Rooms: Vern adds drama and romance to a living room by painting the walls golden yellow, hanging brown draperies, building an armoire with red upholstered door panels, slipcovering the furniture in white fabric dyed with tea bags, and constructing red candle torchères. Laurie tries to convince her homeowners that she can warm up a bedroom with parchment-color paint, soft white and blue fabrics, various chocolate brown accents on the furniture and headboard, and painted partition screens.

Guy Thing: Vern's male homeowner sits down at the sewing machine and is confused about how to make it "go."

Guy Thing, Part 2: When Ty doesn't have time to make Vern's upholstered armoire doors, Vern and the male homeowner go out to the shop to make them by themselves.

Yucky Moment: Paige catches a large fish while standing in a fish market during the introduction.

Reveal-ing Moment: Both of the female homeowners dislike their rooms. In fact, the bedroom homeowner hates her room and keeps talking about all the work she'll have to do the next day to change it.

Vern's Room: 🙂 😐 🙁

Laurie's Room: 🙂 😐 🙁

Seattle: 56th Place

Cast: Paige, Hildi, Genevieve, Ty

The Rooms: Hildi entirely covers a basement rec room in magenta and taupe fabric hung from the ceiling. She also builds new coffee and side tables and slipcovers new sofas with magenta fabric. Gen creates an Asian living room, using shimmery silver and red paints and coating one wall in a metal paint that oxidizes to a rusted finish. She makes a valance out of an obi and uses cedar flowerpots as picture frames.

Conflict: Gen meets opposition when she reveals her Asian theme to her homeowners. They state that their neighbors hate Asian decor.

Navel Alert!: Paige exposes her navel while modeling Gen's organza fabric.

Oops!: While Gen and Paige are crafting a lamp, they recount all of the bad things that have happened when they work on projects together. While lamenting all the things they've broken, Paige slips with the glass globe she's cleaning and breaks it. Gen states, "This is a show of human errors."

Notable: Hildi surprises her homeowners by spray-painting the existing upholstered furniture magenta. Later, one of Hildi's homeowners brings Paige in with her eyes closed and then reveals the painted furniture. Paige is shocked and says that it looks bad.

Budget Crisis: Hildi arrives on Day 2 to find that the tarp blew off the freshly painted furniture; the furniture has been rained on and ruined. Paige eventually agrees to break the rules, letting Hildi go severely over budget in order to buy new furniture. Hildi leaves, and returns with two new sofas (total cost: $500) that are eventually slipcovered.

Hildi's Room: ☺ 😐 ☹

Gen's Room: ☺ 😐 ☹

Oregon: Alyssum Avenue

Cast: Paige, Hildi, Genevieve, Amy Wynn

The Rooms: Hildi cozies a bedroom by upholstering the walls and ceiling with silver-blue fabric, building a bed from storage cubes, draping sheer white fabric from the ceiling center over the bed corners, hanging a chandelier above the bed, and adding a blue monogram to white bed linens. Gen adds a graphic touch to a living room by painting the walls bright yellow, covering a wall with 6-inch squares, building cedar shelving under the stairs, and hanging clotheslines to display art and photos.

Girl Power: Hildi's female homeowner learns how to use the nail gun and is afraid of hurting Amy Wynn with it.

Fashion Report: Hildi's hair is in a ponytail for most of Day 1.

Never-Ending Project: Gen's wall of squares requires a ridiculous number of steps. The design calls for more than a thousand squares of wood, all of which must be specially cut; each square has to be stacked on top of others to create different heights; and the stacked squares must be glued together, stapled to reinforce the glue, primed, painted, hung on the wall, and puttied over to cover the nail holes.

Hildi's Room: ☺ 😐 ☹

Gen's Room: ☺ 😐 ☹

Oregon: Alsea Court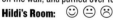

Cast: Paige, Frank, Laurie, Amy Wynn

The Rooms: Frank goes south of the border in a kitchen by painting a serape on the ceiling, making a basket-weave wall treatment with sheet metal strips, painting the cabinet door center panels silver, designing a distressed tabletop, and upholstering dining chairs with serape fabric. Laurie brings warmth to a living room by painting the walls amber, using several expensive fabrics in warm harvest shades, building a long armoire with gold filigree door insets, and designing a large central ottoman.

Quotable Quotes: Frank: "If I see one more howling coyote wearing a bandanna, so help me, I'm gonna run amok."

Frank again: "I feel very Carmen Miranda-ish. Now, quick, get me a pineapple drink and a funny hat."

Conflict: Frank's homeowners question most of his decisions. After fighting to nix a wall decoration late on Day 2, Frank hits a breaking point and says, "I'm going to go fix myself a beverage. You can put those anywhere you want to. The suggestions are numerous, but I won't get into them right now."

Budget Crisis: When Laurie returns the morning of Day 2, she finds that she has run out of brown paint. She still needs to paint the ottoman and finish painting the armoire, but she's out of money. She says, "I'm really kinda stressed about this."

Frank's Room: ☺ 😐 ☹

Laurie's Room: ☺ 😐 ☹

Portland: Everett Street

Cast: Paige, Doug, Vern, Amy Wynn

The Rooms: Doug transforms a family room into an Art Deco theater by painting the floors and ceiling chocolate brown, covering the walls with chocolate brown fabric, building graduated platforms for silver chairs, suspending the television from the ceiling, and installing aisle lights. Vern creates a cohesive look in a living/dining room by painting the walls sage green and hanging sage draperies with white satin stripes on the windows and the walls of the dining area. He also builds a custom armoire and buffet with square wooden insets stained various colors and creates a custom lampshade with handmade art paper.

Fashion Report: Doug wears a knit skullcap; Vern's hair is especially spiky.

Conflict: Doug's homeowners continually question whether there will be room for a computer in the finished design. By the morning of Day 2, Doug is weary of fending them off and mixes a glass of antacid. One of the homeowners again asks him where the computer is going, and Doug points out, rather forcefully, that it will stay in the room.

Guy Thing: Vern explains stuffing a pillow and mounting a wall sconce to his male homeowner by relating these processes to taxidermy, the homeowner's hobby.

Doug's Room: ☺ 😐 ☹

Vern's Room: ☺ 😐 ☹

Santa Clara: Lafayette Street

Cast: Paige, Frank, Laurie, Ty

The Rooms: Frank adds a festive touch to the living room of a Delta Gamma residence by painting the walls two shades of a peachy orange; highlighting the curved ceiling with stenciled stars, triangles, swirls, and dots; painting the sorority letters above the fireplace; and installing a window bench seat. Laurie updates the Delta Gamma chapter room by painting the walls a muted seafoam, stenciling yellow anchors on the walls, designing a coffee table with hidden additional seating, and making a candelabra out of a captain's wheel.

Paint Fun: Frank reveals the wall colors by having both the sorority sisters close their eyes, dip their hands in the paint, and then smear it on the wall.

Word Lesson: While crafting with his sorority team, Frank says "cattywampus," and they question him about whether he made up the word.

Notable: Frank does a cartwheel during the sped-up footage of his team removing furniture from his room.

Go, Girl: Laurie reminisces about her sorority days as a Kappa and talks about having to dress up like Carmen Miranda and sing "Kappa, Kappa-cabana" to the tune of Barry Manilow's "Copacabana."

Acting!: Paige pretends to be a surprised sorority sister at the last Reveal and starts screaming and hugging the sorority members.

Budget Crunch: Over budget by 11 cents, Laurie presents Paige with that amount during Designer Chat.

Frank's Room: ☺ 😐 ☹

Laurie's Room: ☺ 😐 ☹

California: Corte Rosa

Cast: Paige, Vern, Laurie, Ty

The Rooms: Vern gives a bedroom an exotic resort decor by painting the walls light chino, upholstering the bedside tabletops with faux leather, adding tribal- and safari-print fabrics to the draperies and bed linens, hanging a red glass light fixture, and building storage cabinets on a large plant ledge. Laurie creates romance in a bedroom by painting the walls sage green, hanging a French tester canopy above the bed, painting the existing furniture mocha brown, installing a window seat with storage cabinets, and hanging dark green draperies.

For Fun: Vern, Laurie, and Ty pedal tiny three-wheeled bikes at the start of the show.

Fashion Report: Laurie ends her all-black clothing period by wearing a lime green shirt.

Quotable Quote: Commenting on the romance of his room, Vern says to Paige during his Designer Chat, "If this doesn't produce a third child, this is gonna be a total failure."

Notable: Typically mellow Ty is stressed much of the episode and falls behind on his carpentry work.

Vern's Room: ☺ 😐 ☹

Laurie's Room: ☺ 😐 ☹

California: Grenadine Way

Cast: Paige, Vern, Frank, Ty

The Rooms: Vern looks to vintage Indian fabrics for inspiration in a bedroom. He paints the walls soft blue, lays wood laminate flooring, installs a large headboard of basket-woven iridescent fabric, and hangs amber glass candleholders. Frank gives ethnic flair to a living room by painting a mantel with lines of mustard, white, taupe, and black, designing a large wooden sculpture, and building a new coffee table, armoire, and valance.

Get Well!: Vern has laryngitis this episode and is often barely able to speak. He tells Ty on Day 1 that he's doing his best Darth Vader impersonation. By the morning of Day 2, he has to communicate with his homeowners by writing on pieces of paper.

Conflict: Frank's homeowners question most of his decisions, and he adapts most aspects of his design as a result.

Quotable Quote: Frank describes for Paige how he feels about staying under budget, saying simply, "I'm puffed."

Navel Alert!: Paige exposes her navel twice, but you have to really watch for it. The first time is right before the first commercial break; the second time is during the end credits as she balances on Frank's valance, pretending to be a gymnast.

Notable: Penny-wise Vern is over budget (!) by $2.47.

Vern's Room: ☺ 😐 ☹

Frank's Room: ☺ 😐 ☹

Berkeley: Prospect Street

Cast: Paige, Doug, Genevieve, Ty

The Rooms: Doug cleans up the Delta Upsilon fraternity chapter room (and goes "DU-clectic") by painting the walls lime green, installing bench seating, constructing two huge circular ottomans upholstered with lime and orange fabrics, and suspending a tabletop from the ceiling. Gen adds classic Hollywood-style glamour to the Alpha Omicron Pi sorority chapter room by painting white and silver stripes on the walls, adding black and silver throw pillows, building a large armoire, and commissioning her team to trace silhouettes of Paige and herself for wall art.

Fashion Report: Doug dons leather pants (and a crisp blue oxford shirt, of course). Paige sports black, horn-rimmed glasses at the start of the show.

Yucky Moments: Doug is amazed by how filthy his assigned room is. When it's time to clear the room, Doug starts pitching everything out the third-story window—including the sofa. Later, he has his team put on biohazard gear to sweep and clean the room before they start redecorating.

Quotable Quotes: It's all Gen in this episode. Gen tells her eager team members that she wants to create "a couch that screams 'Sexy, sexy, sexy!'" Later, Gen refers to the existing artwork in the room as something "straight out of the lobby at the women's clinic."

Diva Fit Details: When Doug points out that one of his team members missed a spot while painting, she paints his shirt. A full-fledged paint fight ensues.

Conflict: Doug's team fights to keep the existing beer lights in the room, rejecting the custom lights Doug wants to make. Doug eventually gives in.

Budget Busters: Gen calls around to buy a large carpet remnant for her room. When someone quotes her $500, she aggressively bargains down to $275. Both Gen and Doug end up going over budget.

Doug's Room: ☺ 😐 ☹
Gen's Room: ☺ 😐 ☹

Oakland: Webster Street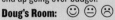

Cast: Paige, Hildi, Genevieve, Amy Wynn

The Rooms: Hildi experiments in a living room by covering the walls with straw. She also installs a wall of bookshelves, covers the fireplace with copper mesh and glass rods, and screens the windows with wooden louvered blinds. Gen brightens a kitchen by painting the cabinets yellow and the walls cobalt blue, building a tile-top island and kids' table, personalizing dishware with family art and photos, and designing a backlit display shelf for a glass bottle collection.

The Last Straw: Hildi's wall treatment turns out to be high-maintenance. She and her homeowners spend much time brushing off straw that didn't adhere and hand-trimming long pieces.

Quotable Quote: Hildi is truly amazed when one of her homeowners explains that the kids who will live in the room may tear straw off the walls and eat it. Hildi questions the homeowner's concern by asking, "Do they eat lint off of the sofa?" The homeowner tells her the children do. Hildi then asks, "Do they walk around outside and eat grass?" The homeowner tells her they do indeed.

Fashion Report: Gen has her hair wrapped in numerous tight little buns à la Scary Spice. One of her homeowners uses a hair bun as a pincushion while sewing. Gen lets her hair down for her Designer Chat, to voluminous effect.

Reveal-ing Moments: The living room homeowners seem to like the design but are unsure about having straw on the walls with two young children in the household. When they demonstrate how the kids will pick at the straw, Paige eats two small pieces of straw. One homeowner swears after seeing the wall treatment and has to be bleeped.

Hildi's Room: ☺ 😐 ☹
Gen's Room: ☺ 😐 ☹

California: Peralta Street

Cast: Paige, Hildi, Doug, Amy Wynn

The Rooms: Hildi divides a living room into quadrants by painting two opposite corners of the room and ceiling silver and painting the remaining corners and ceiling space violet. She supplements the look with a clear-glass mosaic on the fireplace surround, four industrial-style chairs, and a large circular ottoman upholstered in silver and violet. Doug thinks pink in a dining room. He paints the walls bubble gum pink, paints the ceiling chocolate brown, hangs a lamp upside down from the ceiling, upholsters new white dining chairs with lime green T-shirts, and tops new storage units with green gazing balls.

Musical Moments: In this tuneful episode, the four homeowners play together in their band as Doug and Hildi dance together at the start of the show. Later, Doug attempts to rap, and Hildi plays guitar badly while assigning homework

to her team. For the finale, Doug's male homeowner sings a song to Amy Wynn to entice her to do the necessary drywall work in the room. She refuses.

Oops!: Hildi attempts to drill through four large stones so she can attach them as legs on her ottoman. That doesn't work, so she has to use an adhesive to connect them.

Yucky Moment: Hildi photocopies parts of her own body to make wall art.

Nasty Side: Doug throws all the homeowners' knickknacks into the trash at the start of the show. Doug then reveals his paint colors to his homeowners by splashing the paint on a wall à la Jackson Pollock. Later, Doug gets personal by delving into his homeowners' relationship (they've split up but they're still working on the room together).

Notable: During her Designer Chat, Hildi claims her room is one of her favorite designs ever.

Hildi's Room: ☺ 😐 ☹
Doug's Room: ☺ 😐 ☹

Los Angeles: Willoughby Avenue

Cast: Paige, Doug, Genevieve, Ty

The Rooms: Doug sees red in a living room: He stencils the walls and doors in red and white, using a rectangular graphic based on a pillow pattern. He paints the ceiling gray, lays a red shag rug, and builds a U-shape couch with red upholstery. Gen designs a swingin' living room with 1950s flair by painting the walls aqua, covering floor stains with black paint, transforming mod place mats into wall sconces, slipcovering a futon in white vinyl, and laying a bookcase on its side to create a new coffee table.

Fashion Report: Gen wears a Britney Spears-inspired tube sock on her arm during Designer Chat. Doug's leather pants make another appearance, and Doug appears to be growing a goatee.

Off-Key: Doug and his team sing loudly to annoy Gen's team, who is working in the room directly above Doug's.

Back Atcha: Gen's team throws an old TV down the stairs to get back at Doug's team for singing so loudly. Paige and Doug convince Doug's homeowners that the noise was caused by the big-screen TV being accidentally dropped down the stairs. When the homeowners rush out to see the damage and realize it was a joke, one of them says, "Yea! Fun on the Learning Channel! Fun for everyone!"

Safety First!: When Paige and Gen go to a local flower market to buy orchids late on Day 2, Gen runs across the street without looking both ways.

Flaming Success: Gen lights a cigar with a blowtorch when her room comes together and her team members announce they're done.

Gen's Design Theory: "I think it's important whenever you do something that's remotely hip...that you are able to update. Otherwise you're stuck in something that becomes very passé."

Conflict: Ty has too many projects and calls an executive meeting with Paige, Doug, and Gen. Doug agrees to give up a ceiling installation project so Ty will have time to finish Gen's projects.

Reveal-ing Moments: Both male homeowners swear during The Reveals and have to be bleeped.

Quotable Quote: During the end credits, Doug's male homeowner does a fine Paige impression, saying, "Hi, America. I'm Paige Davis. Look at my cute little Sandy Duncan hair."

Doug's Room: ☺😐☹
Gen's Room: ☺😐☹

Los Angeles: Springdale Drive

Cast: Paige, Vern, Laurie, Ty

The Rooms: Vern brightens a dining room by painting the walls yellow, hanging bronze draperies, installing a wall-length buffet with built-in storage, and designing a multi-armed halogen chandelier with gold vellum shades and a

hanging candleholder. Laurie enlivens a basement den by painting the walls yellow, slipcovering the existing furniture with natural cotton duck fabric, sewing an aqua Roman shade, installing several yellow and aqua shadow box shelves, designing a folding screen to mask exercise equipment, and painting squares and rectangles in various shades of aqua to create custom wall art.

Oops!: Vern's homeowners write positive thoughts on the walls in pencil, with the intent of painting over them as they work on the room. The writing shows through the paint, and they have to go back and clean off what they wrote before they finish painting the room.

Guy Thing: Vern and Ty have a great deal of trouble bringing in the buffet. It's too long to make several of the turns in the house, and they bump the corner of it on a doorway, scuffing the piece.

Vern's Room: ☺ 😐 ☹
Laurie's Room: ☺ 😐 ☹

California: Abbeywood Lane

Cast: Paige, Frank, Hildi, Ty

The Rooms: Frank gives a living room a cohesive look by painting the walls sage green; building an upholstered wall hanging in shades of peach, coral, and yellow; painting a life-size image of the homeowners' toddler on the wall; making throw pillows out of fabric designed by the homeowner; and crafting candleholders out of 4×4s covered with license plates. Hildi creates her version of a nautical living room by painting the walls black; nailing 120 lightly stained 1×2s on the walls in a vertical arrangement about 2 inches apart; building two large mirror-image couches; using seafoam fabric to upholster the couch, create throw pillows, and make draperies; and mounting photos of the ocean onto blocks of wood.

Oops!: Ty demolishes the existing pass-through in Frank's room and takes a chunk of the wall with it.

Jokester: Frank tricks his homeowners by telling them that his design involves painting primitive sage-colored figures on the existing yellow walls. The homeowners look at the large cow Frank has painted and start painting images of their own. A few minutes into it, Frank tells them that he lied and that they're going to paint the entire room sage.

Notable: Paige and Frank "kiss" while wearing dust masks.

Frank's Room: ☺ 😐 ☹
Hildi's Room: ☺ 😐 ☹

Austin: La Costa Drive (celebrity episode)

Cast: Paige, Vern, Hildi, Ty

The Rooms: In the first celebrity episode of *Trading Spaces*, Vern breathes life into the bonus room of Dixie Chicks lead vocalist Natalie Maines. Vern paints the walls yellow, installs a wall-length desk and sewing unit, hangs a huge chandelier, and sews throw pillows, draperies, and bed linens with shimmery red fabric. Hildi adds style to a sewing room, which belongs to Natalie's mother, by railroading gray and sage fabric on the walls, installing wooden louvered wall dividers, building a 14-foot couch, reupholstering a vintage shampoo chair with sage chenille, and covering a coffee table with slate tiles.

Call-In: Ty is too busy to come over to Vern's room during Day 1, so Vern phones in his measurements to him.

Quick Chick: Hildi and Natalie have a sewing race while working on the couch bolsters. Natalie wins.

Remember When?: Hildi's homeowners joke that they had hot dates the night before and couldn't finish their homework, alluding to Doug's homeowners in the New York: Sherwood Drive episode from Season 1.

Oops!: Ty burns out his table saw on Day 1 and can't work on anything for a while.

Vern's Room: ☺ 😐 ☹
Hildi's Room: ☺ 😐 ☹

Texas: Sherwood Street

Cast: Paige, Frank, Genevieve, Amy Wynn

The Rooms: Frank transforms a kitchen by removing strawberry wallpaper, sponge-painting a focal point wall, hanging new draperies with a pear motif, painting the avocado green floor and countertops with faux tiles, and hanging a thin plywood sunburst around the existing fluorescent light. Gen conjures a New England cottage feel in a bedroom by painting three of the walls pale smoke, painting one of the walls ultrabright white, building a fireplace mantel-style headboard, creating curtain tiebacks from red neckties, sewing bed pillows from pinstriped suit jackets, distressing the existing ceiling fan, and adding a library nook.

Quotable Quote: Frank calms his homeowners' fears of a new painting technique by saying, "I will take you by the hand, lead you to the river of paint, dip you in it, and baptize you to the great religion of faux finishes."

Groovin': Paige briefly breakdances on Frank's rug during sped-up footage of the team moving furniture back into the room.

Conflict: Gen's homeowners beg her not to hang moss on the walls. She assures them that she is not planning to.

Resourceful: Near the end of Day 2, Gen pulls in a stone bench from the garden because she can't afford to buy one.

Reveal-ing Moments: The kitchen homeowners love their room so much they won't stop screeching. Paige eventually puts her fingers in her ears.

Frank's Room: ☺ ☺ ☹
Gen's Room: ☺ ☺ ☹

Houston: Sawdust Street

Cast: Paige, Laurie, Doug, Amy Wynn

The Rooms: Laurie refines a living room by painting the walls margarine yellow, building a wall-length bookshelf, hanging bamboo blinds and yellow drapery panels, and adding two spicy orange chairs. Doug goes "Zen/Goth" in a living room by painting the walls blood red, building an L-shape couch, hanging a large wrought-iron light fixture, and blowing up a photo of the female homeowner in lingerie and knee-high boots to hang over the fireplace.

Notable: Laurie announces that she is pregnant.

Oops!: Laurie's homeowners do such a bad job painting the bookshelf that Laurie has them scrape off the paint and redo it.

Sketchy: Doug draws his couch design for Amy Wynn on toy magnetic drawing board.

Resourceful: Doug uses a pool noodle to create bolster pillows for the couch. There's a sequence of scenes showing him stealing it from kids in the pool area, who chase after him, yelling, "Give me back my noodle!"

Stirring Moment: Doug's homeowners are supposed to paint the fireplace black for their homework. They don't do the assignment, because when they opened their paint can, they thought the paint looked blue. Doug demonstrates that paint needs to be stirred.

Yucky Moment: Doug finds the revealing photo to hang over the fireplace by digging through the female homeowner's drawers.

Payback: Doug is nearly $50 over budget; he pays Paige in cash during his Designer Chat.

Laurie's Room: ☺ ☺ ☹
Doug's Room: ☺ ☺ ☹

Houston: Appalachian Trail ✳

Cast: Paige, Doug, Laurie, Amy Wynn

The Rooms: Laurie adds style to an office/playroom by painting the walls terra-cotta, building a large shelving and desk unit with plumbing conduit, painting the existing coffee table and armoire in eggshell and black, adding new seating, and creating the illusion of symmetry with cream

---

draperies on an off-center window. Doug goes for a soft look in a bedroom by painting the walls pale blue, upholstering a tall headboard in blue chenille, sewing new blue and white bed linens, and installing custom light fixtures.

Yes, She's Pregnant: Confirming her announcement in a previous episode, Laurie holds her stomach much of the episode.

Conflict: Laurie starts painting the artwork for the room without her male homeowner and Paige, telling them that she's worried about time. When Laurie leaves the room, Paige tells the homeowner that she knows Laurie too well to believe that Laurie was worried about time, adding that Laurie wanted "to control the final product."

Fashion Report: Doug appears to suddenly have a fair amount of gray hair.

Name Game: Doug titles his room "A Pretty Room *by Doug*" (and yes, the italics are important).

Cheer Up!: Doug's female homeowner is a cheerleading coach. Her squad appears in the driveway and does a cheer for Doug: "Fix that space. You're an ace. Go, Doug, Go. You're a pro." Perhaps inspired by the cheerleading, Doug does a cartwheel later in the show.

Doug's Room: ☺ ☺ ☹
Laurie's Room: ☺ ☺ ☹

Plano: Bent Horn Court

Cast: Paige, Genevieve, Vern, Ty

The Rooms: Gen regresses as she designs a playroom, painting multicolor polka dots on the walls, cutting movable circles of green outdoor carpeting for the floors, building a large castle-shape puppet theater, hanging fabric-covered tire swings, and designing four upholstered squares on wheels, with storage space inside. Vern gets in touch with his rustic side in a living room by laying natural-color adhesive carpet tiles, painting an existing armoire and other furniture pieces black, and building a combination ottoman/coffee table/bench unit.

Fashion Report: Paige, Gen, and Ty all wear cowboy hats at the start of the show.

Go, Girl: Gen sends Paige on a mission around the house to find objects with different textures that Gen can frame and hang as kid-friendly art.

Oops!: Ty makes Gen's wheeled squares at the last minute, and she doesn't have time to paint them. The tops are upholstered, but the sides are bare fiberboard during the Reveal.

Gen's Room: ☺ ☺ ☹
Vern's Room: ☺ ☺ ☹

Plano: Shady Valley Road

Cast: Paige, Hildi, Doug, Ty

The Rooms: Hildi creates a two-tone bedroom by painting the walls bright white, installing 12-inch orange baseboards, building a new head- and footboard that match the pitch of the cathedral ceiling and covering them with white slipcovers, and upholstering a chair with white faux fur. Doug adds sophisticated style to a playroom by painting the wall moss green ("Moss Madness"), installing beams on the ceiling in a barnlike formation, building a basket-weave armoire, revamping a futon into a daybed, and hanging bifold doors on a toy closet.

Gifted: The two female homeowners are budding interior designers and have a business making draperies, table runners, and lamps. They present Paige with a small lamp during the key swap.

Conflict: Hildi plans to dye the carpet in her room orange, but her female homeowner is adamantly opposed to the idea. They have several discussions about dyeing the carpet, with the homeowner becoming increasingly forceful in her opposition. At one point, Hildi asks rhetorically why she's been asked to design the room if she's not going to be allowed to follow through on her vision. Then she notes, "Everyone in America knows I can rip up that carpet if I want to." Hildi gives up at the end of Day 1, and the carpet stays

---

white. (She problem-solves by sprinkling orange flower petals across the carpet for the Reveal.)

Notable: Doug and his female homeowner go fabric shopping with the PaigeCam at the end of Day 1.

Hildi's Room: ☺ ☺ ☹
Doug's Room: ☺ ☺ ☹

Texas: Sutton Court

Cast: Paige, Laurie, Frank, Ty

The Rooms: Laurie designs a kitchen, using the homeowners' china for inspiration. She paints the walls taupe with white trim, builds large wooden shadow boxes to display china pieces, hangs new light fixtures, and uses taupe fabric for the window treatments and chair cushions. Frank works with a Southwest theme in a living room, adding chamois-cloth accents to the existing furniture, building a footstool out of a saddle, hanging several custom-made art pieces, designing a Mission-style armoire, and making potted cactus out of vegetables.

Blah: Laurie's paint choices don't create a bold effect—the dining area is already the same shade of taupe as her main paint color and the kitchen trim is already the same shade of white.

Money Woes: Laurie and her homeowner are laying two rugs when Paige comes in to say that Laurie is already significantly over budget. Laurie doesn't believe it until Paige tells her that the wood cost twice as much as expected. Laurie sadly agrees to return the rugs to the store.

Notable: Frank is hoarse throughout the episode and tells Paige, "I sound bad, but I am so perky."

Laurie's Room: ☺ ☺ ☹
Frank's Room: ☺ ☺ ☹

Raleigh: Legging Lane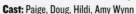

Cast: Paige, Frank, Hildi, Amy Wynn

The Rooms: Hildi adds romance to a bedroom by painting the walls slate gray, hanging smoky plum draperies, sewing a tufted lavender coverlet, framing a favorite picture of the Eiffel Tower, and building cubic bench seats and nightstands. Frank lets his creativity flow in a playroom by painting walls, furniture, doors, and floors in a multitude of pastel colors. He also hides a large refrigerator, builds an armoire to house media equipment, and designs a large toy chest.

Ceiling A-Peeling: Hildi's popcorn-texture ceiling starts flaking in several places; attempts to fix it fail.

Oops!: When Paige brings the homeowners into Hildi's room for the Reveal, she accidentally leads the male homeowner into the TV stand, banging his leg.

Paint Explosion!: Frank uses paint in every shade of the rainbow—and then some.

Frank's Room: ☺ ☺ ☹
Hildi's Room: ☺ ☺ ☹

North Carolina: Southerby Drive ✳

Cast: Paige, Doug, Hildi, Amy Wynn

The Rooms: Doug adds an Eastern touch to a bedroom by painting the walls china blue and painting white chinoiserie murals. He builds a black four-poster bed with PVC pipe, adds a custom-built sculpture, hangs white draperies, and paints the furniture black. Hildi also displays Eastern influences in a bedroom, painting the walls a soft green and installing a wall of shoji screens to create a headboard. She covers the screens and the existing furniture with lavender crackle finish, hangs lavender draperies, and upholsters with purple fabric.

Resourceful: Doug creates the murals by placing an image on an overhead projector, sketching the image on the wall in chalk, and painting in the image with white paint.

Quotable Quote: Hildi's female homeowner says to her while upholstering, "Why did I ever doubt you, Hildi?"

Doug's Room: ☺ ☺ ☹
Hildi's Room: ☺ ☺ ☹

Wake Forest: Rodney Bay

Cast: Paige, Vern, Laurie, Amy Wynn

The Rooms: Vern adds drama to a bedroom by painting the walls gray, attaching a fabric canopy to the ceiling, designing a headboard with interior lights that shine out of the top, painting the existing furniture black, and upholstering a chair with gray flannel. Laurie brightens a living room by painting the walls a bold shade of green, installing two floor-to-ceiling shelving units with crown molding, hanging yellow draperies, adding several pillows in warm harvest shades to the existing off-white sofa, and hanging a new parchment-shade light fixture.

Oops!: Vern and Amy Wynn have several problems transforming a dresser into a desk. First, Amy Wynn cuts the drawer fronts too small. Then she installs the top so that the drawers aren't accessible. Vern is upset with Amy Wynn's work and tells Paige, "This is not a viable workable solution." They have to reinstall the top.

Yucky Moment: The upholstery on the existing off-white couch is extremely soiled. Laurie freaks out because she had been told that the couch was in good condition and she planned her whole design around it. She and her homeowners spend hours scrubbing the couch with heavy-duty cleaner and brushes.

Quotable Quote: In order to convince her homeowners that she must remove the existing ceiling fan, Laurie states, "I cannot in good faith do this room and not do this."

Reveal-ing Moments: Both sets of homeowners love their rooms, but the male living room homeowner swears twice upon opening his eyes and finding that the ceiling fan is gone. He vows to hang it up by the next morning.

Vern's Room: ☺ ☺ ☹
Laurie's Room: ☺ ☺ ☹

Season 3

Maine: George Road ❓

Cast: Paige, Doug, Genevieve, Ty

The Rooms: Doug adds warmth to a kitchen by painting the walls umber, painting the woodwork white, installing a butcher-block countertop, building a large pantry unit with bifold doors, and sewing a large tablecloth. Gen updates a dark kitchen by painting the walls bright green, installing a black and white tile countertop, building a butcher-block island, hanging wood laminate wall paneling, and installing a 1930s light fixture.

Quotable Quotes: Doug's female homeowner tells her husband that Doug is "easy on the eyes." She goes on to say, "He hasn't been a real jerk yet."

Yucky Moments: Doug, Ty, and Paige make several laxative and lubricant jokes because the new countertop has to be rubbed with mineral oil.

Girl Power: When Gen's male homeowner gets a bit too excited about working with a pretty young woman, Gen takes control of the situation, telling him, "If I can handle power tools, I can handle you."

Awful Wall: Gen covers a large wall in laminate paneling that's supposed to resemble worn wooden planks. Isn't this the sort of thing that gets painted over by *Trading Spaces* designers?

Creature Feature: Ty and Doug attempt to put live lobsters in Gen's hip waders during B-roll footage.

Budget Boasting: When Gen learns her budget is at $776.52, she looks into the camera and says, "Beat that, Doug!"

Doug's Room: ☺ ☺ ☹
Gen's Room: ☺ ☺ ☹

Portland: Rosemont Avenue

Cast: Paige, Laurie, Vern, Ty

The Rooms: Laurie goes nautical in a living room by painting the walls deep aqua blue, painting the fireplace white, putting a cream-tone paint wash on wooden chairs and upholstering them with zebra-print fabric, and installing a vintage mercury glass chandelier. Vern brightens a living room by painting the walls yellow, hanging black and yellow Roman shades, installing French doors, covering the ceiling with white steel squares, hanging a ceiling fan, using black slipcovers for the existing furniture, and adding silver fold-up trays to serve as side tables and a coffee table.

Conflict: Laurie struggles with the placement of a piano in her room. The home belongs to musicians who enjoy playing in their living room, but the floor joists aren't strong enough to hold the piano where Laurie wants to put it. She decides to leave the area empty and moves the piano to another room.

Design Insight: Laurie says this is the first time that her paint color choice on *Trading Spaces* was not inspired by fabric. (Her inspiration in this case was the name of the paint color, which refers to the bay where the episode was filmed.)

Time Crunch: Vern falls behind in his room because he and Ty have a difficult time installing the French doors.

Notable: Vern actually installs an all-white ceiling fan in his room! He points out that it's a *Trading Spaces* first.

Laurie's Room: ☺ ☺ ☹
Vern's Room: ☺ ☺ ☹

Maine: Joseph Drive 😈 ❓

Cast: Paige, Laurie, Frank, Ty

The Rooms: Laurie enlivens a bedroom by painting the walls soft yellow, building an Asian-style shelving unit, designing a new headboard, sewing gray and white toile bedding, and adding an unusual floral light fixture. Frank shows another side of his design style in a bachelor's bedroom. He paints the walls and ceiling dark blue-green, hangs simple white draperies, sews a large plastic envelope to hold a pencil drawing of a leaf on the wall, builds a table that houses three wooden bins, and jazzes up a rocking chair with pet collars.

Notable: This is Laurie's last show before having her baby.

Fashion Report: Paige has short hair. The flip is gone.

Conflict: Although painting the headboard was one of the homework tasks Laurie assigned, her homeowners are only starting to prime the piece on the morning of Day 2. Laurie wanted to do a faux finish but can't because the paint won't be dry in time.

Quotable Quote: Frank, on his room design: "I want this to be the pit of wild monkey love."

Really?: Frank repeatedly tells anyone who will listen that this room will not contain any faux finishes or distressed objects. When Paige challenges him and says that he'll paint a chicken somewhere, he claims that he's only painted a chicken once in the history of *Trading Spaces*.

Laugh Riot: Frank and one of his homeowners make custom candleholders with metal pipe nipples and flanges. The homeowner becomes giggly at the mention of pipe nipples, and she and Frank can't stop laughing throughout the project. When Frank talks about the varying lengths of pipe nipples that are available, he says, "They come in all sizes, just as in life."

Huh?: Frank has his homeowners make art pieces with tar paper. He tells them he wants them to paint "a cave painting of a person who is very geometrically neat."

Yucky Moment: Frank straps pet collars on an existing rocking chair, explaining coyly that they can function as arm and leg restraints for visitors to the bachelor pad.

Laurie's Room: ☺ ☺ ☹
Frank's Room: ☺ ☺ ☹

Long Island: Steuben Boulevard 🔌 ☹

Cast: Paige, Edward, Frank, Ty

The Rooms: Edward jazzes up a bedroom by painting the walls light mocha, hanging wall sconces, building an Art Deco armoire, painting Deco patterns on the closet doors, installing lights around the bottom edge of the bed frame, hanging a canopy, and painting a faux-malachite finish on the furniture tops and wall sconces. Frank gets woodsy in a dining room, painting the walls deep orange, installing pine doors between the dining room and kitchen, creating a coffee table out of a large flowerpot, painting white birch trees all around the room, and making a large pig-topped weather vane to sit above the fireplace.

Notable: Edward makes his designer debut in this episode.

Fashion Report: Paige looks as if she stepped out of the cast of *Li'l Abner* with a Daisy Mae-inspired top.

Oops!: Ty and Edward talk extensively about the armoire for Edward's room, but they can't agree on the dimensions. The finished piece ends up being too tall for the room, and Edward cuts off the feet to make it fit.

A Compliment?: Ty finishes installing the bed light, turns it on, and tells Edward, "It looks like Vegas!"

Getting Personal: Frank admits to a fear of heights.

Name Game: Frank names the weather vane pig "Poopalina."

Shopping Savvy: Frank describes the bargain-hunting skills he used to purchase a rug at a home store: "I pitched such a walleyed fit about [the store] not having one wrapped in plastic that they gave me a 10 percent discount."

Edward's Room: ☺ ☺ ☹
Frank's Room: ☺ ☺ ☹

Long Island: Split Rock Road ❓

Cast: Paige, Genevieve, Vern, Amy Wynn

The Rooms: Gen brightens a dark kitchen by painting the walls white, the trim celadon green, the window shutters pale blue, and the cabinets yellow. Gen also polishes the existing copper stove hood, hangs white wooden slats on one wall, builds a butcher-block table, skirts the dining chairs in white fabric, and coats a new light fixture with copper spray paint. Vern adds a soft touch to a kitchen by painting the walls and cabinet door insets green, painting parts of the cabinet doors white, stenciling white fleurs-de-lis on the cabinet doors, building a new laminate countertop, laying a two-tone parquet floor, using green toile fabrics on Roman shades and table linens, adding touches of green gingham to the tablecloth, and adding several green-shaded table lamps to the countertop.

Dance Break: Gen dances to shake a can of spray paint.

What Was She Thinking?: Wanting to make candleholders out of pieces of rock, Gen tries to drill into the rock with a carbide bit that she was assured could handle the job. (Didn't she remember the California: Peralta Street episode in which Hildi had similar problems?!) After several attempts, Gen looks into the camera and says, "I suggest buying candleholders at the local hardware store."

What Was He Thinking?: The small table lamps that Vern places on the countertop have to be plugged in, so cords are still strewn everywhere during The Reveal.

Notable: Gen's inspiration for her design is a necklace that the homeowner wears nearly every day. One of Vern's homeowners is the woman featured in the Swiffer ad that airs with the Season 3 episodes.

Gen's Room: ☺ ☺ ☹
Vern's Room: ☺ ☺ ☹

New York: Whitlock Road

Cast: Paige, Genevieve, Doug, Amy Wynn

The Rooms: Gen designs a bedroom with an espresso color scheme: She paints the walls café au lait, uses darker java on the ceiling beams, and paints sections of the ceiling cream. She also sews orange asterisks on a white bedspread, builds a combination headboard/desk, and exposes original wood flooring. Doug updates a bedroom by painting squares on the wall in multiple shades of sage, building a mantel-like headboard, designing S-shape side tables, sewing stripes of yarn on a white bedspread, and framing strips of wood veneer for bedside art.

Fashion Report: Paige wears a tank top or, rather, several matching tank tops featuring phrases that relate to each scene of the show: Key Swap, Blue Team, Red Team, Gen, and Doug.

Conflict: Gen's male homeowner fights her on every decision. Gen points out that they wouldn't have to argue about every choice if they would let the designer decide. They eventually wear her down, and she tells them to fight between themselves and pick a ceiling color; she'll do whatever they want. Later, when her male homeowner is complaining about her fabric choices, Gen mouths to the camera that after two days she'll be out of there and won't have to listen to him.

Conflict, Part 2: Doug's homeowners fight him on the bed placement. He wins.

Yucky Moment: Gen and Amy Wynn shoot an air compressor hose into their mouths, blowing out their cheeks.

Faux Arrest: During the end credit shots, Paige is handcuffed by a local police officer.

Budget Boasting: Gen's total costs amount to $763 and some change—the lowest budget quoted on camera thus far in the series.

Gen's Room: ☺ 😐 ☹
Doug's Room: ☺ 😐 ☹

New York: Half Hollow Turn

Cast: Paige, Frank, Kia, Amy Wynn

The Rooms: Frank brings a living room up-to-date by painting the walls bamboo yellow, adding black accents on the walls and the furniture, using concrete stepping-stones to create side tables, converting a garden bench into a coffee table, and hanging a custom sculpture made from electrical and plumbing components. Kia gets funky in a basement rec room by painting the walls purple and light green, building a wall-length bench with purple velvet upholstery, hanging a swirly purple wallpaper border, installing halogen lights on a running cable, and creating green draperies.

Notable: This is theme queen Kia's first episode on the show.

Quotable Quotes: Frank describes his design idea as "transitional, cautious, contemporary." After assigning homework, he tells his homeowners, "I will skulk out of here like the creep that I am and leave you to this horrible work."

Budget Crisis: Paige uses too much spray paint on Frank's concrete stepping-stone project, but Frank doesn't have the money to buy more paint. Paige goes to Amy Wynn to figure out whether they can return enough of Frank's wood to buy the paint.

Conflict: One of Kia's homeowners fights Kia's decision to hang vertical blinds. Kia returns on Day 2 with fabric to create draperies instead.

Yum!: After the final Reveal, one of the homeowners presents a cake with the entire *Trading Spaces* cast airbrushed on the frosting.

Frank's Room: ☺ 😐 ☹
Kia's Room: ☺ 😐 ☹

Philadelphia: 22nd Street

Cast: Paige, Edward, Genevieve, Ty

The Rooms: Edward adds ethnic flair to a living room by painting the walls red, texturing the fireplace with black paint and tissue paper, hanging an existing rug on the wall, building a chaise lounge with finial feet, and installing an entertainment center made of shadow boxes. Gen heads to Cuba in a bedroom by covering the walls with textured white paint, adding a faux-plank finish to the doors, building a headboard enhanced with a blown-up image from a Cuban cigar box, designing lighted plastic bed tables, and creating picture frames out of cigar boxes.

Edward's Design Theory: "You always have to have a grounding force of black in the room."

Notable: Gen's inspiration for her room is the entire country of Cuba. She's never been.

Quotable Quote: Gen: "When you're working with a $1,000 budget, you've got to faux it up a bit."

Fashion Report: Gen wears a knee-length skirt and kitten heels while decorating her room.

Edward's Room: ☺ 😐 ☹
Gen's Room: ☺ 😐 ☹

Philadelphia: Gettysburg Lane

Cast: Paige, Frank, Vern, Ty

The Rooms: Frank updates a kitchen by painting the walls and cabinets several different colors, laying a stone-look vinyl tile, installing a new countertop, adding decorative elements to a half-wall to create a new serving bar, and mounting plates with wooden food cutouts across the soffit. Vern adds his version of cottage style to a living room by painting the walls yellow, installing white wainscoting, building a 12-foot-wide shelving and storage unit, framing large copies of old family photos, making a "quilt" of images to hang above the storage unit, and adding touches of denim fabric throughout the room.

Fashion Report: Vern shows off his legs by wearing shorts.

Quotable Quote: Frank's male homeowner tries to get out of faux-finishing, suggesting that it's a job for a woman. Frank says, "All of a sudden I feel like I have to go out and buy a dress for the prom because I do this all the time."

Time Crunch: Vern gets an unexpected head start on his room because the homeowners removed the existing wallpaper before the *Trading Spaces* team rolled into town. (The homeowners were afraid Vern would paint over the wallpaper.)

Yawn: Vern gets virtually no sleep between Days 1 and 2 because he's trying to help finish the built-in storage unit.

Yucky Moments: Ty has a running gag of using wood glue as lotion, rubbing it into his hands, face, and neck.

Frank's Room: ☺ 😐 ☹
Vern's Room: ☺ 😐 ☹

Pennsylvania: Gorski Lane

Cast: Paige, Frank, Doug, Ty

The Rooms: Frank adds a celestial touch in a bedroom by painting the ceiling deep plum and painting silver stars across it. He paints the walls with several shades of cream and green, adds small blocks of color to the paneled doors, builds a writing desk, hangs a small cabinet upside down on the wall, and makes several pieces of custom artwork. Doug brings some "jungle boogie" to a bedroom by painting zebra stripes across all four walls, painting the ceiling dark brown, suspending a bamboo grid from the ceiling, and covering the existing headboard with sticks and bamboo.

Road Rage: During the opening, Doug and Frank ride four-wheelers through a field. Frank wears a little blue helmet and pulls Ty behind him on a skateboard. Ty eventually falls off, and Frank stands next to him as Doug zooms by, indifferent to Ty's predicament. Frank shakes his head and mutters, "The compassion of a speed bump." Adds Ty, "Will someone get a rock and hit him in the head?"

Fashion Report: Doug shows off his legs by wearing shorts and flip-flops. There are also several buttons undone on his shirt.

Quotable Quote: When Frank unveils his purple paint, he says to his homeowners, "Prepare yourselves for the final squeal."

Oops!: While Ty is helping one of Frank's homeowners install a ceiling fan, Ty's drill falls from his ladder and lands on the fan, shattering the glass. Frank rushes into the room and is speechless. Ty and the homeowner try to blame each other as Ty goes to stand in the corner. Ty eventually buys a new ceiling fan, paying for it himself so that it doesn't come out of Frank's budget.

Conflict: One of Doug's homeowners is very concerned about covering the walls with zebra stripes. As she tries to talk him out of doing it, Doug says, "There's no way you're gonna stop me, so don't even try."

Resourceful: Doug wants to include a table but doesn't have extra money in his budget to pay for lumber. Ty ends up digging through the trash for scrap timber to make it.

Frank's Room: ☺ 😐 ☹
Doug's Room: ☺ 😐 ☹

Long Island: Dover Court

Cast: Paige, Vern, Edward, Amy Wynn

The Rooms: Vern sets a boy's bedroom in motion by painting the walls various shades of blue, building a race car bed with working headlights, suspending a working train track and toy planes from the ceiling, hanging a motorcycle swing made from recycled tires, and hanging precut letters on the walls to spell out words like "woosh" and "zoom." Edward brings the outdoors into a bedroom by painting the walls moss green and antiquing a landscape print above the bed. He alters prefab side tables with filigreelike cuts, disguises ugly lamps with black spray paint and fabric slipcovers, hangs antique glass shutters over the windows, and builds a large entertainment center, using the existing side tables and more glass shutters.

Notable: Paige skateboards during the opening segment. Vern's homeowner keeps saying "sweet," and Vern tries to claim the word is his.

Resourceful: Having heard that Vern is doing a "planes, trains, and automobiles" room, neighborhood kids want to give him pictures of all three to hang in the room. Vern likes the idea but points out that he doesn't have the money to pay them. The kids donate the pictures, which Vern then incorporates into the room.

Confession Time: While sewing, Edward's male homeowner admits that his wife is better than he is with power tools.

Vern's Room: ☺ 😐 ☹
Edward's Room: ☺ 😐 ☹

Pennsylvania: Victoria Drive

Cast: Paige, Doug, Kia, Amy Wynn

The Rooms: Doug creates a cabin feel in a living room by covering the walls in soft brown Venetian plaster, hanging red Roman shades, covering a prefab coffee table with leather, staining the existing sofa and coffee tables a darker color, sewing cow-print throw pillows, building a large armoire covered with rough-cut poplar, and hanging leftover lumber on the walls in decorative stripes. Kia creates her version of an indoor garden in a guest bedroom by painting the walls yellow, hanging a flowery wallpaper border on the ceiling, creating a duvet out of synthetic turf and silk flowers, building a headboard from a tree limb, hanging a chair swing from a cedar arbor, placing gravel under the swing, and building a picket fence room divider.

Fashion Report: Doug dons a cowboy hat in several scenes. In keeping with the theme of her room, Kia wears overalls and a straw hat.

Yucky Moment: When Doug's homeowners enter the room to meet him at the start of the show, Doug is barefoot, sitting on a window seat and enjoying a plate of brownies left for all of them by the other homeowners. Doug offers to share, but his team turns down the offer because Doug's feet are close to the plate. Doug then taps his foot across the top of the brownies and offers them again. He pushes the grossness even further by sticking a piece of brownie between his toes and trying to shove it in their faces.

Quotable Quote: While staining the existing tables, one of Doug's homeowners expresses her relief that they aren't painting them. Doug retorts, "I would not damage anything of quality. I only damage things that are crappy."

Impressive Impersonation: Kia does her best Gary Coleman by saying, "Wha'choo talkin' 'bout, Amy Wynn?"

Oops!: The first cedar arbor that Amy Wynn builds for Kia's swing is too big to fit through the bedroom door, and Amy Wynn can't take it apart without ruining it. Kia doesn't have the budget to buy more cedar, so Amy Wynn pays for the extra wood to create a second arbor inside.

Doug's Room: ☺ 😐 ☹
Kia's Room: ☺ 😐 ☹

New Jersey: Manitoba Trail

Cast: Paige, Frank, Doug, Amy Wynn

The Rooms: Frank goes all out in a country living/dining room by painting the walls light green, distressing the floors, painting a faux rug under the coffee table, applying several decorative paint colors and finishes to an antique cabinet, building custom lamps with large antique yarn spools, and creating three homemade country-girl dolls out of pillow forms. Doug brightens a living room by painting everything—the walls, ceiling, ceiling beams, fireplace, and ceiling fans—bright white ("White Whoa"). He buys two new white sofas, hangs bright blue draperies, installs a new doorbell that blends into the white wall, sews many brightly colored throw pillows, makes a large framed mirror, and creates custom art pieces.

Quotable Quote: Because one of his homeowners is experiencing soreness in her neck and shoulders from a recent accident, Frank tells her to go rest; he says he'll stay and do her homework. Frank then puts on her homeowner shirt and impersonates her, saying, "I can't believe that little, fat, rotund twerp gave us all this homework after we worked all that time."

Foot Fetish: Doug goes barefoot while painting a white border on a natural rug and puts his bare feet near his female homeowner's head while she sews pillows.

Reveal-ing Moment: The male country living/dining room homeowner is so happy about his room that he kisses Paige on the cheek.

Frank's Room: ☺ 😐 ☹
Doug's Room: ☺ 😐 ☹

Nazareth: First Street

Cast: Paige, Vern, Doug, Amy Wynn

The Rooms: Vern adds a touch of serenity to a living room by painting three walls taupe and one wall deep blue, adding a new mantel, sewing throw pillows with a wave motif, suspending mini symbiotic environments from the ceiling, building a coffee table with a center inset of sand and candles, and placing six fountains around the fireplace. Doug gives a kitchen an earthy feel by laying brown peel-and-stick vinyl flooring, painting the walls beige, making new orange laminate countertops, painting the cabinets yellow with an orange glaze, adding crown molding to the cabinet tops, building a pie safe, and upholstering the dining chairs with red-orange fabric.

Fashion Report: Vern's pants fall down as he's running during the opening segment. Doug wears a do-rag while laying the peel-and-stick flooring.

Earthy Inspiration: Vern's sand-and-sea design springs from the homeowners' love of the beach and the desert.

Notable: Amy Wynn and Doug have a food fight during the end credits.

Vern's Room: ☺ 😐 ☹
Doug's Room: ☺ 😐 ☹

New Jersey: Catania Court $

Cast: Paige, Hildi, Genevieve, Amy Wynn

The Rooms: Hildi has the golden touch in a bedroom: She paints the walls yellow-green, sews bedding with fabrics she purchased in India, uses batik-inspired stamps to create gold accents on the ceiling and around the room, replaces the existing baseboards with taller ones, adds a gold wash to the existing furniture, builds a low-slung "opium couch," and hangs a vintage glass light fixture. Gen finds the silver lining in a dining room: She paints the walls carnelian red, hangs silver crown molding, paints the trim and chair rail ivory, hangs ivory and silver draperies, paints a canvas floorcloth to lay under the table, and hangs a new light fixture that has small tree limbs attached to it.

Fashion Report: Hildi's male homeowner starts the show wearing heels, noting that he's chosen "Hildi-approved footwear." Hildi paints his toenails with the room paint. When the homeowner starts to take off the shoes in order to paint, Hildi tells him to put them back on, pointing out that she never goes barefoot on the job.

Ringing Inspiration: Gen gets her design idea from a piece of her own jewelry, a ring that came from Afghanistan.

Oops!: Gen keeps cutting wallpaper strips too short to hang on the walls. She eventually says, "Only serious professionals need apply for this job!"

Hildi's Room: ☺ 😐 ☹
Gen's Room: ☺ 😐 ☹

Philadelphia: East Avenue ?

Cast: Paige, Hildi, Frank, Amy Wynn

The Rooms: Hildi gets graphic in a living room by painting three walls yellow, covering one wall with a large Lichtenstein-inspired portrait of herself, adding a glass-shelf bar area, building all new tables and chairs, sewing cushions with mod pink and orange fabric, and re-covering a thrift store couch with red fabric. Frank brightens a living room by painting the walls deep purple, painting the ceiling bright red, designing a coffee table unit with four bases that move apart and become extra seating, and creating wall art with rain gutter materials and round wooden cutouts.

Notable: All four homeowners are members of the Philadelphia Charge, a professional women's soccer team.

Fashion Report: Paige wears her most conservative outfit ever: black pants, tennis shoes, and a red soccer jersey.

Stormy Weather: An overnight storm ruins Hildi's lumber, throwing all her projects into peril. (Great shades of Hildi's spray-painted couch episode!)

Time Crunch: Throughout the episode, Paige tries to track a package of accessories that Frank shipped from Texas. The package doesn't arrive until late on Day 2.

Resourceful: After applying one coat of purple paint on the wall, Frank realizes that the original burgundy paint is showing through in patches, creating an unexpected faux finish. He decides to keep it that way.

Quotable Quote: While hanging draperies, Frank dispenses his wisdom, saying, "A little fluffing is good."

Reveal-ing Moments: The homeowners are "weirded out" by the Hildi portrait in their freshly painted yellow living room.

Hildi's Room: ☺ 😐 ☹
Frank's Room: ☺ 😐 ☹

Virginia: Gentle Heights Court $ ☹ ♥

Cast: Paige, Hildi, Kia, Ty

The Rooms: Hildi roughs it in a boy's bedroom by painting the walls and ceiling midnight blue, hanging a moon-shape light fixture, placing glow-in-the-dark stars on the ceiling, hanging a solar system mobile, building a 13-foot rock climbing wall, adding several pieces of fold-up camping furniture, placing the mattress in a room-size tent, using a blue sleeping bag as a duvet, and placing camping lanterns around the room. Kia adds sensuous details to a bedroom by painting the walls orange, painting the trim Grecian blue, hanging a red and gold wallpaper border, creating a Taj Mahal cutout to place around the existing entertainment center, installing two wooden columns from India, adding bedding made from sari fabrics, and suspending the bed from the ceiling with chains.

Guy Stuff: Ty (wearing a bike helmet for safety, of course) and Hildi's male homeowner try out the completed rock wall. They fall on top of each other on the floor.

Quotable Quote: When Kia asks Ty when he's going to hang the chains for her bed, he says, "Just as soon as you're through yanking mine."

Midnight Carpentry: Ty must work late into Day 1 to complete Kia's Indian column project. He uses the PaigeCam to record himself working (and complaining about the fact that he is working).

Notable: A shirtless Ty suns himself during the end credits.

Reveal-ing Moments: Upon seeing the suspended bed in her newly decorated room, the female homeowner exclaims, "I wanna jump in there and get naked!"

Hildi's Room: ☺ 😐 ☹
Kia's Room: ☺ 😐 ☹

Arlington: First Road 😈 ?

Cast: Paige, Hildi, Doug, Ty

The Rooms: Hildi gift-wraps a bedroom by painting the walls "Tiffany box" aqua blue, adding a duvet and Roman shades in the same aqua blue, airbrushing white "ribbons" on the walls and fabrics, hanging white lamps with square shades above the headboard, building acrylic side tables that light up from inside, and adding bright silver accents. Doug warms up a bedroom by painting the walls and ceiling a deep gray-blue, hanging white Roman shades with brown silk curtains and cornice boards, constructing a headboard from a large existing window frame, balancing the headboard with a new armoire that features white silk door insets, and creating custom artwork in brown and navy.

Homework Blunder: For homework, Hildi has her team airbrush the "ribbons" on the walls. When she returns on Day 2, the project is complete but not quite the way she would have done it. (The "ribbons" are very large and look more like Keith Haring-inspired graffiti.) Hildi tries to keep a positive attitude and says (not too convincingly), "It's fine."

Notable: One of Hildi's homeowners leaves an apology note on the wall in black marker. It says, "Hildi made me do it."

Conflict: Doug's homeowners fight him on every decision, including removing the ceiling fan, selecting paint colors, painting the ceiling, staining the floor, and accessorizing the room. At one point, Doug tells them, "I've done 30-some *Trading Spaces* episodes. I know what the hell I'm doing." Near the end of Day 1, Doug washes his hands of the room and uses the PaigeCam to record instructions for making draperies. Paige then takes the camera to the homeowners and helps them make the curtains.

Quotable Quote: At a heated point in the conflict with his homeowners, Doug exclaims, "I can't continue to educate people on what's good taste!"

Reconciliation?: While Doug is reclining in a lawn chair reading a newspaper, his homeowners come to say that they need him after all. By the end of Day 2, Doug's female homeowner admits that the design is growing on her. Doug says, "It's growing on her like a fungus, but it's growing."

Hildi's Room: ☺ 😐 ☹
Doug's Room: ☺ 😐 ☹

stay tuned...

Coming August 2003—2 new books!

Trading Spaces
COLOR!

Trading Spaces
CUSTOM TOUCHES!

Let *Trading Spaces* inspire your next decorating project and teach you how to do it just like the show's designers!

Turn to this new *Trading Spaces* how-to series for cutting-edge design advice on:

* Paint
* Fabric
* Accessories
* Color
* Furniture
* And much more!

Each title in this how-to series will:

* Boost your decorating confidence with inspirational room photography
* Help you get your act together without breaking the bank
* Give lots of helpful planning tips and purchasing strategies
* Create cool, custom looks that fit your style and personality

Look for them wherever quality books are sold!